DICHOTOMY

AMISH JUSTICE!

Beverley and Stan Jolley

Penn  Press

Woodland Hills, California

Published by
Penn Press
PMB 291
22106 Clarendon St.
Woodland Hills, California 91367-9780

Publisher's Cataloging-in-Publication Data
Jolley, Stan.
    Dichotomy ♦ Amish Justice!: 2000.
        p. cm.
    ISBN 0-9674877-0-6
            1. Amish—Pennsylvania—Fiction. 2. Farm life—
    Pennsylvania—Fiction. I. Jolley, Beverly. II. Title.
PS3560.055 D53   2000
813'.54—dc21   99-64740

PROJECT COORDINATION BY JENKINS GROUP, INC.

October 1999

03 02 01 00 ♦ 5 4 3 2 1

Printed in the United States of America

Lovingly Dedicated to:

Our FAMILY and FRIENDS . . . .

Who never lost faith

in

"DICHOTOMY ♦ *AMISH JUSTICE!"*

and

to our

devoted Pennsylvania believers.

We thank you one and all.

Bev and Stan

Chapter 1

It is a warm summer evening in the peaceful Amish community of Lancaster, Pennsylvania. The silence of the night gives way to the sound of dogs barking in the distance, crickets chirping, and the soft whirring of windmills as they slowly turn in the gentle breeze.

Only when one has entered this almost unpenetrable community, of a barely understood culture that has basically never changed in over three centuries, can one appreciate the eerie silence of no sounds from the maddening pace of a technology driven world.

It is as if God dropped an invisible curtain around the measured acres of rolling hills and farms for protection from the evils of modern day intrusions.

Silhouetted and creeping silently against the late night sky, two dark figures wend their way up a grassy embankment toward one of the sleeping farms. No doubt, they are intruders of the night. Suddenly one of them stops, strikes a match, and lights what looks like a crude Molotov cocktail, then throws it through the air.

The burning fuse and bomb fly toward an Amish barn, shattering the tranquility of the night with a deafening explosion, as the end of the barn ignites in flames. The other figure, now silhouetted even more by the blaze, hurls another lighted device at the far end of the barn. The violent eruption and fire is horrendous. The outline of the two men race toward a wide-bodied pickup truck waiting on the dirt lane leading to the country road.

Inside the Amish barn, the frightened animals react in fear as the end of the barn becomes aglow with the beginning of a roaring fire. Sows are squealing, trying to gather their piglets around them, horses in wild-eyed terror are rearing in their stalls and pawing the air while screaming their fear, and cows in panicked fright are trapped in their milking stalls. The sounds of slamming truck doors and screeching tires is heard over the confusion.

Outside, the Amish barn is now a roaring inferno with the desperate cries of the animals piercing through the sound of the crackling fire. The pickup, with its lights off, disappears down the dark, desolate road.

From the farmhouse, with its multiple extensions, a

large Amish family rushes out of the various structures and runs toward the barn. The elders shout urgent instructions to the younger men, women, and children to rescue the animals. The mother grabs the rope to the bell tower and frantically begins yanking it, sending the tolling message of an emergency to their neighbors.

The barn doors are pulled open as the desperate family enters the burning barn. They quickly begin to lead terrified animals to safety.

The pickup creeps up a lane to another Amish farm. In the background on the ridge, the glow of the burning barn is seen. The ominous figures quickly emerge from the pickup truck and repeat their heinous actions, only with more precision and haste. Once again at breakneck speed, the pickup departs down the lane to the highway, with that barn also going up in flames.

In a very short time, several barns in the distance are ablaze and lighting up the night sky.

Inside a typical sparse Amish bedroom, Hans and Rebecca Ammann awaken.

As is the required Amish custom, Hans has given up the clean-shaven face of bachelorhood and wears a

3

handsome full beard. His face, though somewhat weathered from working in the fields since childhood, has a gentleness about it, with eyes that cannot mask an inner kindness. He is a tall man of slender build, with strong physical strengths that belie his looks.

His own father died when he was a youth of twelve, thrusting family responsibilities upon him at an early age. Being the eldest of six children, he stepped quickly into the role of family leader, which is the Amish tradition, eventually gaining the respect of the community and becoming a Deacon in the church.

Rebecca, in spite of the motherhood of four children, is still very attractive of face and figure. Her beautiful dark hair falls softly around her shoulders framing her large blue eyes. Though traditionally all Amish women wear their hair pulled tightly back in a bun, at bedtime they are allowed to let it down. Because the women never cut their hair, Rebecca's falls well down to her waist in thick, wavy curls. There is almost a saintly glow around her innocent face, in spite of the fact that Amish women wear no makeup or embellish themselves in any way.

They hurriedly leap out of bed to the clanging of the farm bells ringing through the night air alerting the Amish community of the need for their help.

The flickers of the eerie fire dance on their bedroom walls. Hans and Rebecca, in their nightclothes, quickly go to the window and see the glow of a burning barn over the immediate horizon.

"It's on the Stoltzfus' farm!" Hans cries out.

He quickly crosses to the bedroom door and yells loudly down the hall to his son.

"Matthew! Matthew! Wake up!"

Matthew is sound asleep in his bedroom. He is seventeen and a wholesome young lad. Even though on the verge of manhood, he has a beautiful innocence and clean chiseled features with large, dark eyes. His thick brown hair is shoulder length, which is not unusual for young male Amish youths. His smile is broad and contagious and people are naturally drawn to him because of his gentle and kind ways. Tall and slender, he also shows the strength of having worked on the farm and labored at traditional family chores.

Matthew struggles to wake up when he hears his father's voice.

"Matthew, get the buggy harnessed . . . the Stoltzfus' need help! They got fire!"

Rubbing his eyes in confusion, Matthew hurriedly starts getting dressed.

Jacob, Matthew's little four-year-old brother, flies out of the other bed and runs into the hallway. He races down the hall and practically knocks down his two sisters, Elizabeth, nine, and Mary, six, who in their nightgowns have come out of their bedrooms to see what all the commotion is about. Jacob plows through them and enters his parents' room.

Hans, now dressed, is putting on his shoes. Jacob and the excited girls enter and rush to their mother.

Jacob pleads to her, "I want to go, too! I want to go . . . I can help!"

Now turning to his father, hoping he'll accept his plea, he asks, "Can't I, Father?"

Rebecca gathers her little tyke to her and holds him close. Hans, now dressed, rushes toward the door and yells back to her, "Rebecca, take care of the children! We'll be back by milking, I'm sure."

On the way out, Hans tousles his son's hair affectionately, and grabbing his hat, hurries down to the barn. "Next time, Jacob."

"Be careful, Father!" Elizabeth pleads anxiously.

"God's speed, Hans," Rebecca calls after him.

Outside the Ammann farmhouse, the pristine Amish farm reflects the closeness to nature and strong affinity for the soil and hard work. Matthew rushes out the front door, tucking in his shirt and slamming on his hat as he runs to the barn.

Matthew is startled when he throws open the barn door to find his grandfather, Ezra Ammann. Ezra, his hair and beard thin and his body gnarled with age, hasn't lost his efficiency and is just finishing harnessing the horse to the buggy.

"How did you . . . ?" Matthew questions.

Ezra quickly starts to lead the horse out of the barn. "You'll find, Matthew, when you get older . . . old men don't need much sleep. I guess the good Lord figures we'll get all we need soon enough."

Hans comes running up and takes the reins. They quickly climb into the buggy. Matthew tries to help his proud grandfather, but Ezra keeps slapping his assisting hands away.

The buggy races up the lane and Jacob runs out of the house, waving and chasing it with all the exuberance of a four-year-old boy. Concerned and confused, Grandma Ammann halfway waves from her doorway.

From the bedroom window, Rebecca hugs Elizabeth and Mary close to her. They watch the Amish buggy race up the road as the blazing glow over the hill creates a tableau of a seventeenth century Dutch master's painting. Silhouetted on the crest of the hill, Jacob, in his nightshirt and with his little Amish hat on, waves at the disappearing buggy in the orange-red flickering glow.

Chapter 2

At the Stoltzfus' burning barn, there is mass confusion as the animals are being released. Women and children lead them to safe pastures as Amish buggies and wagons arrive from all directions, loaded with helping hands and crude equipment.

An old, outdated fire engine with siren blaring arrives on the scene with the local volunteer non-Amish firemen aboard. They start unloading hoses and equipment, with their voices raised to a fever pitch over the roaring noise of the fire.

In the background, from over the hill and cutting across the field, Hans is urging his horse and buggy on at a frenzied pace. Ezra and Matthew hang on tightly as they hit ruts and bumps.

From the buggy they can see the frantic effort being made to save the barn, now completely enveloped in flames. Leaping down when they reach a rail fence. Hans ties off the horse. Matthew and Ezra jump down and begin to help the firemen drag hoses.

Speeding down the lane, a sleek newsreel truck pulls up and the efficient crew starts unloading and setting up equipment, lights, and cameras. In no time they have picked the most interesting angle, with the barn blazing in the background.

The cameraman focuses on a sophisticated young female newscaster. She begins talking into her microphone. "Ladies and gentlemen, I'm Donna Heckler. We're here in the heart of this fascinating Amish community in Lancaster County, Pennsylvania, where they've had a rash of senseless barn burnings, but nothing on the scale of tonight."

She gestures to the activities. "As you can see in the background, several barns along this country road are ablaze. Why anyone would want to do harm to this quaint Amish sect, who forsake all modern conveniences while devoted to intense religious vows, is a complete mystery to local and state authorities."

Nearby, a frustrated fireman, whose face is already covered with soot, growls, "Well, if they'd just halfway join the twentieth century and at least get telephones, we might have been able to save a few of these barns."

He starts to put away some of the equipment for it is obvious to him there is nothing they can do to save the barn. The Amishmen and firemen start to back away from the roaring inferno.

Matthew passes by carrying a stray, frightened little calf in his arms. The aggressive newswoman grabs his arm and nods to her cameraman, while his assistant turns the light and camera on Matthew.

"Young man, I'd like to . . ." Donna eagerly begins to interrogate her captured prey.

Matthew throws one hand up in front of his face to hide from the camera while the determined, pushy newscaster starts to pull his arm down, anxious to continue questioning him.

"I was just going to . . ."

Just then Hans steps in front of the camera with his back to it, blocking it from photographing Matthew and himself. "Please respect our ways and privacy . . . no pictures . . . the Bible says 'Our graven image' . . ."

At that moment a dirty and tired Ezra takes Hans and Matthew in tow and leads them away from the newsreel crew. "You don't have to explain, Hans . . . come, let's go home. We can't do anymore until tomorrow."

The frustrated newswoman nods to her cameraman and he switches back to her. "As you just saw, the Amish are really not concerned with the outside world or how the outside world perceives them. Their religion is a total way of life, with their sanctions deeply rooted in a disciplined and pacifist existence. This is Donna Heckler from Lancaster County, Pennsylvania."

Chapter 3

The next morning at the Stoltzfus' house and barn, true to their communal beliefs and strict scriptures, the Amish are taking care of one another in this time of need. The area is a beehive of activity. The barn is nothing but charred remains, with Amish men tearing down what's left. Ezra is directing Hans with his horse dragging a makeshift rig as he pulls ashes and debris into piles.

Matthew and a group of his friends are loading horse-drawn wagons that are hauling the debris away.

The Amish women, all similarly dressed in their white bonnets and dresses cut from the same pattern, are setting up tables on the lawn in front of the house.

Rebecca is helping organize the unloading of the food baskets and supervising Elizabeth and Mary, who are helping along with the other girls. All of the children, true to the Amish custom, are dressed like miniature versions of their parents.

Grandma Ammann is on the porch swing with her quilting project while watching and gossiping with the other older women sewing in their rocking chairs. They wouldn't think of just being idle, for they truly believe "Idle hands are the devil's workshop."

Jacob is doing what all four-year-olds do, imitating the older men; but in reality, he is mischievously playing games and having fun, while annoyingly under foot.

Amos King, David Beiler, and Joseph Miller, along with Matthew, are dirty and sweaty with black soot on their clothes and faces as they take a slight break from shoveling.

Amos King is excited and conspiratorially whispering to his friends.

"She's a beauty of a heifer . . . I just got her two days ago!"

David, under his breath, says anxiously, "I can hardly wait!"

Joseph, in eager anticipation, asks, "Where do you have her?"

Amos turns to Joseph and confides, "Down at the Strasburg Pike, near the Yoders. Tonight you're coming with us, Matthew . . . No?"

Matthew, concerned and struggling, looks over at Hans who is taking a breather with Ezra. An attractive

Amish girl, Sarah, is ladling out water in glasses to them. She looks over and smiles at Matthew and the boys, but Matthew, not noticing, shrugs to Amos. "That's a long way . . ."

Amos proudly replies, "Not with her speed at all."

Now David chides in, "Awe, Matthew, you gotta' loosen the harness."

Matthew starts to lead the horse and full wagon away, struggling with his decision. "I don't . . . oh, I will come."

Amos whispers excitedly to his friends, "We'll meet at the covered bridge at seven."

Sarah is taking the glass back from Hans. He smiles and nods. "Thanks, Sarah, that beats Schnapps any-time."

Ezra savors the last drop of water, laughs, and hands back his glass. "Thank you, Sarah."

Ezra apprises her. "You've become such a young woman so quickly. Hasn't she, Matthew?"

Matthew is just passing by, leading the horse and wagon. Sarah blushes at Matthew and obviously is attracted to him, but Matthew's thoughts are elsewhere.

"Ah, what, Grandfather?"

Ezra is nodding his head up and down behind Sarah enthusiastically. "Sarah's become a woman right before our eyes, yah?"

Matthew turns to shyly take a real look at Sarah. He fumbles for words. "Ah, yes, Grandfather . . ."

Hans is about to say something but Ezra quickly takes his arm, "Come Hans, it's back to work." Ezra quickly leads Hans away, leaving a deathly silence between Matthew and Sarah.

Blushing, she finally finds her tongue. "Would you like some water, Matthew?"

"Yah, thank you, Sarah." Matthew heaves a sigh of relief for the welcomed distraction.

Sarah begins to ladle him a glass of water.

On the Stoltzfus' front porch, the old women, smiling as they work, are obviously watching Matthew and Sarah. Grandma Ammann calls to Rebecca, who is busy nearby. "Ah, Rebecca . . ."

She nods toward Matthew and Sarah with an all-knowing twinkle in her eye. "It looks like it's time for Matthew to *bei-schlof!*"

All the older Amish women titter as they watch Rebecca, Mary, and Elizabeth look over at Matthew and Sarah. Rebecca responds with a surprised smile and a twinge of concern. "Yah, Grandma Ammann, maybe you're right."

Matthew has finished his water and turns to lead the horse away. "Thank you, Sarah."

Sarah is disappointed he's not pursuing the opportunity and says impatiently, "Matthew?"

He stops and turns. "Yah?"

Sarah, desperately fishing for words, says, "Ah . . . ah, it's Saturday night . . . I mean tonight!"

" . . . Yah, Sarah?"

Now that she's started, Sarah doesn't know how to follow up with no response at all from Matthew. She stammers and is now flustered, almost beyond words. "Ah . . . do you have a good flashlight, Matthew? I mean, well, if you would be so inclined, I'd be . . ."

Now it's Matthew's turn to be embarrassed. His face is beet red, for he well knows the customs of the Amish. He also fumbles for words. "Sarah . . . ah . . ."

Then relieved, he remembers. "Sarah, I'm going over to Amos King's tonight with David and Joseph."

Sarah is disappointed but now is relieved that her boldness, which was even a surprise to her, finds her off the hook. Matthew, aware of her feelings and his mixed emotions, quickly responds, " . . . but Sarah, thanks for the invitation . . . maybe in the future."

Ezra is smiling and nudges Hans as they sneak another glance over at Matthew and Sarah.

On the porch, Rebecca, Mary, Elizabeth, and the old women are trying hard not to watch as they see Matthew head their way. He turns and waves a good-bye gesture to Sarah. Now buoyed by Matthew's last remark, she perks up, waves, and smiles coyly back.

Matthew approaches the porch deep in his own thoughts, unaware that he is being watched. Quickly Rebecca, the old women, and girls busy themselves, trying not to be obvious. Matthew notices his mother and stops for a moment, then calls, "Mother, is it all right if I go over to Amos King's tonight with David Beiler and Joseph Miller?"

Again there are a few little titters from the porch and Rebecca is having a hard time keeping a straight face. "If that's what you really want to do, Matthew."

Matthew looks back at Sarah, who is now giving Amos and the boys water at the wagon they are loading. Now Matthew really has mixed emotions. He just nods and starts to lead the horse and wagon away.

Mary and Elizabeth can't contain themselves any longer. They quickly race to their brother and teasingly dance around him, taunting and playfully singing.

Elizabeth loudly begins chiding him. "We know where you're going!"

Mary now chimes in with her sister. "We know where you're *really* going!"

Laughingly, Elizabeth raises her voice another octave. "And we know what you're going to do!"

Now both girls are jumping up and down in front of Matthew. "To do . . .to do . . . to do . . . !"

Matthew, embarrassed and a little annoyed, playfully swats the loose reins at them. "No you don't . . . now go away!"

Realizing the girls are out of control, Rebecca calls to them in as stern a voice as she can muster, all the while trying to contain her own smile.

Matthew speeds up the horse's gait and the girls giggle and skip back to Rebecca, who can't contain her smile any longer. Neither can the old women, with their wonderful Amish faces and all-knowing looks, hide the enjoyment and fun of the moment.

Chapter 4

The moon silhouettes a picturesque old wooden covered bridge that's over a lazy meandering stream.

Under a nearby tree, and tied to a low limb, is an Amish horse and buggy. Amos King, David Beiler, and Joseph Miller are anxiously waiting for Matthew. David and Joseph each have a small bundle under their arms.

David, annoyed, keeps looking for Matthew's familiar figure. "Maybe he changed his mind."

"That's not Matthew . . . his word is goot," Amos declares. Then, not so sure, he begins to pace.

Joseph spots the form of Matthew coming down the hill. He, too, is carrying a small bundle under his arm. "Yah, true, there he is . . . let's go."

Amos unties his horse and Joseph and David climb into the back seat of the buggy.

"Hurry Matthew!" Amos anxiously calls.

Matthew trots the last few yards and hops in just as the buggy starts through the covered bridge.

Once inside the buggy, they all put their bundles on the floor and get adjusted.

The horse and buggy gain speed and come out the far side of the bridge. David, heart pounding with excitement, whispers to his friends. "I can hardly wait to see her."

Amos is whipping the reins, encouraging the horse to trot at a faster pace down the country road. A few cars pass the buggy with their lights almost blinding them as they approach. Amos turns to Matthew and confesses breathlessly, "We've decided to go to Philadelphia instead of Lancaster."

David and Joseph adlib their excitement about the adventure.

"I've been to Chester Springs once and that was twenty miles from home," declares David.

"The furthest place for me was Valley Forge and that was thirty-one miles. Grandpa took the whole family!" Joseph proudly proclaims.

Matthew starts to protest. *"Philadelphia!* Don't you think . . ."

Amos, not wanting anything to mar his big secret and adventure, disgustingly snaps at Matthew, "Awe . . . that's your problem, Matthew . . . you *think* too much!"

The buggy is moving along at a good pace when

behind them a speeding convertible loaded with a pack of local punks drinking beer races up and flicks on their bright lights. They come within inches of hitting the buggy as they fly by with the pack laughing.

Amos tries to control the frightened horse from going into the ditch with the buggy. The Amish kids react in fear when they hear the screech of brakes in front of them.

The convertible pulls onto the shoulder of the road and makes a u-turn, anxious to try again. Driving on the wrong side of the road, it comes in the opposite direction straight at the horse and buggy.

A couple of punks are standing up in the convertible and quickly popping open beer cans as they approach. "Move away, you imbeciles!" yells the first one with a maniacal laugh.

The other punk throws his beer can and shouts, "Bombs away! And get those shit-dropping nags out of our way!"

The can flies out of the convertible and hits the road in front of the horse and flies up at the frightened animal. Another beer can is hurled at the buggy.

Inside, through the blur of the oncoming headlights, Amos and Matthew instinctively duck. Amos, in frightened terror, blurts out, "Oh, Joseph — Mary!"

The loaded can splatters and hits the windshield of the buggy, shattering it to smithereens and dowsing the boys with beer and glass. Amos quickly struggles with the horse's reins, trying to keep the terrified animal from going off the road into the ditch. The convertible at the last second veers off, missing horse and buggy by a hair.

The frightened and nerve-wracked boys see the convertible continue to race off down the road with the drunken malevolent hoodlums. They all breathe a sigh of relief as Amos tries to calm the horse. "Whoa, girl, whoa!"

"Why can't they just leave us alone?" Joseph groans with a tear in his voice.

"We didn't do anything to them . . ." David anguishes.

Matthew, perplexed and sad, adds, "I don't understand . . . We don't ask them to join our way of life — why are they so threatened by ours?"

With only the sound of the horse's hooves hitting the pavement, they continue on down the road, silent in their own thoughts as they try to wipe the beer and glass off their clothes.

In the distance, with the usual highway traffic, the horse and buggy approach the Pennsylvania Turnpike. Amos steers the buggy off the road near an isolated shed and tree. He pulls the buggy behind the tree and ties the horse to a limb. Nearby, a tarp with four poles is covering what looks like a small rectangular stack of hay.

The boys pile out, now forgetting their experience. Amos excitedly pulls the poles and tarp off and proudly reveals a modest, inconspicuous "old plug" of a car . . . but to the Amish young men, it's a golden chariot. They "ooh" and "ah" over it.

Amos opens the trunk and takes out a bundle stashed similar to the one the other boys have with them. He opens it, revealing non-Amish city clothes. He starts taking off his broad brimmed black hat, shirt, and pants. The others follow suit, carefully and neatly putting their similar Amish clothes and hats in the trunk of the car.

The boys certainly are not in sartorial splendor and they look and feel awkward in their makeshift English clothes.

Anxiously, they pile into the car.

Amos, with all of the fanfair and attention his new acquisition deserves, puts in the key and turns the switch. The old plug shrugs and shakes alive to the awe of his buddies, who are not at all phased by the tremendous shaking of the car caused by a missing spark plug.

Proudly and confidently Amos puts his hands on the steering wheel then, remembering, puts it in gear. The nag jumps to attention then jolts backward, much to the surprise and fright of its passengers. Amos slams on the brakes, practically taking all their heads off. Then, embarrassed, he puts the car in forward gear and jerks them down the road. The hay burner weaves somewhat erratically as it heads toward the busy Pennsylvania Turnpike.

"Are you sure we should go on the Turnpike, Amos?"

Matthew's anguished question falls on Amos' deaf ears. The charging steed heads up the freeway on-ramp, no match for the modern charging herd bearing down on them.

Chapter 5

Amos, with his newly excited city slicker entourage, is driving slowly down a neon-lit street filled with restaurants, porno shops, bars, and strip joints. Their eyes are in wide amazement seeing girls on curbs and street corners selling their wares and waving at them.

David points to a brilliantly lit strip joint that proclaims to have the best-looking and liveliest strippers in Philadelphia. "Let's go in that one . . ."

"Yah, that's goot, no Matthew?" Joseph eagerly exclaims.

Amos sees a car pulling out at the end of the block. "I can maybe park there."

Matthew offers a weak resolve. "I don't think we should . . ."

"Awe, Matthew, there you go again, thinking."

Amos sighs with great frustration and turns to his

friend in a pleading tone. "This is the only time in our lives the elders ever turn their heads . . . Yah? Before we take our vows . . ."

He erratically pulls in and parks and they all eagerly pile out of the old car.

The boys really look out of step with their ill-fitting clothes and mannerisms as they stare wide-eyed at the scene around them.

Amos, David, and Joseph excitedly approach the entrance with Matthew, who is now not so sure this is all such a good idea and is lagging behind. He is startled when a well-seasoned and endowed hooker, who has been sizing him up, takes his arm and sidles up close next to him. Her bizarre makeup and sexy outfit leave nothing to the imagination.

"First time in the 'Big City,' Honey?" she coos in his ear. Matthew is so caught off guard, embarrassed, and tongue-tied that all he can do is nod, while at the same time stare at her assets.

"I'd be so perfect for a young stud like you."

Matthew is trying to free his arm while she starts to touch his crotch with her free hand and sexily whispers, "Sweetheart, I'll teach you all about 'Cherry Blossom Time' in no time at all!"

She laughs at a beet red and sweating Matthew, who breaks his arm loose and races to catch up to his saviors and buddies as they enter the strip joint.

Just inside the smoke-filled entrance, a huge, tough-looking bouncer stops them. "Licenses?"

The boys look confused and then David and Joseph point to Amos. Matthew finds his voice and offers lamely, "We don't drive."

Amos digs in his pants and produces his license.

"Amish, huh?" The bouncer allows a slight smile as he looks at them.

They shyly nod. The bouncer laughs and winks at a nearby bar girl. "Take my friends here down to the best seat in the house."

A foursome is just leaving a table next to the center of the ramp. The waitress ushers the boys to the now vacant spot. They walk in awe and peek around the smoke-filled room. One of the strippers is just beginning her act and the music bumps, grinds, and blares from the stage.

"What'll it be, boys?" the bar girl asks while seating them.

They're so spellbound looking up at the voluptuous, almost nude, stripper above them, they don't even hear her. Even the hardened waitress allows herself a smile. "To drink, that is."

Matthew realizes she's talking to them, turns, and nudges the others. "Beer . . . four beers, yah?"

David and Joseph barely turn around and nod and then turn back quickly. The big, good natured Amos, fascinated and not wanting to miss a stroke of what is undulating right above his head, just raises his big farm hand with his thumb pointing skyward.

The waitress starts to leave but a young man sitting

at the next table with a raucous group stops her. "Another round for all of us, and especially for my bro here."

He's pointing to a carbon copy of himself, his twin brother. He puts his hand on the shoulder of a handsome young naval midshipman in uniform from Annapolis.

"Todd, I think we've all had enough," the level-headed cadet, Kevin, wisely acknowledges.

Todd replies with a touch of drunken sarcasm. "Come on, Kev old boy, it's not every day we get to celebrate our dad's dream come true . . . another round!"

The waitress takes their order and leaves.

Todd notices Amos at the next table, who is slapping his knee and nudging Matthew, then David and Joseph. Amos is in an exalted state of excitement as the stripper plays up to him.

Todd pokes Dino, a very streetwise, tough-looking kid sitting next to him, and points to the four boys at the adjoining table. "Another group of Amish hayseeds right off the farm."

They all laugh, except Kevin, and turn to watch the stripper.

By now, she has moved over and is in front of Matthew, practically grinding her wares right in front of his face. The crowd is really into it but Matthew, obviously very embarrassed, tries to back up a little. Todd reaches over and pushes him back toward the ramp.

He taunts him. "You're supposed to put some money in her 'G' string, dummy!"

The crowd laughs and Matthew fishes in his pants pocket. He pulls out a crumpled dollar bill and meekly offers it up to the stripper. The crowd playfully "boo's" and Matthew is confused.

Dino reaches over from his table and pushes Matthew's arm up at the stripper's leg and body. "Shithead! Put it next to the other bills!"

The crowd roars as Matthew, with eyes almost closed, puts the bill in her "G" string as her body sexually writhes and undulates next to his shaking hand. Even Amos, David, and Joseph are enjoying Matthew's discomfort.

The bar girl brings the beers and a nervous Matthew downs his almost in one swig. "Want another?" she asks.

Turning to the others, she is surprised seeing them down theirs practically non-stop.

"Yah, goot! Another!" Amos signals and eagerly turns his attention back to the stage.

At the other table, Todd, Dino, and Armando, another tough-looking punk, are getting nasty and begin to loudly and deliberately taunt the Amish kids.

"You're chicken shits, right?" Dino is right in Amos' face.

"You never fight for your country, right?" Armando is nudging Joseph hard in the ribs.

"You never stand up for anything! You're pussy-

31

cats!" Todd baits Matthew. Then adds, looking up at the stage, "Pussy . . . cats! You're not even that! You're just *pussys!*" He maniacally laughs at his own stupid joke.

"Aw, leave them alone," Kevin, disgusted, sighs.

Todd, in drunken sarcasm, turns his attention back to his brother. "Oh, my *goody* two-shoes bro . . . still sticking up for the underdog!"

"Well, I stuck up for you your whole life!" answers Kevin, peeved.

Dino, not paying any attention to the bickering, turns in his chair and thumps Matthew hard on the chest.

Matthew tries to remain passive and ignores him. He turns away, but Dino grabs his shirt and pulls him around back towards him. "What's the matter? Didn't you have a *hot enough* time last week out on the farms that you had to come in here!?"

Todd laughs approvingly at Dino's joke.

A beautiful black woman in her mid-thirties has been trying to perform her number from the stage above them and is getting angry. She hisses down, "Leave them alone and *shut the fuck up!*"

"Fuck you . . . you black bitch!" Dino angrily snarls back.

Instantly, in a rage, the stripper flies off the stage at Dino with her nails out as talons and tears into Dino like a wild tigress. The entire place erupts into a powder keg and a real free-for-all explodes throughout the strip joint.

True to their Amish beliefs, Amos, David, Joseph, and Matthew are pacifists and non-participants, but they are getting the hell beat out of them. Amos, just protecting himself from Dino, has been wrestled to the door where the bouncer throws them both out on the sidewalk.

They both stagger and Amos accidentally trips and falls on top of Dino. The huge farm boy passively has him spread-eagled on the sidewalk and Dino is having a hard time freeing himself. From the distance they can hear the sound of sirens getting nearer.

"Get up you dumb shit . . . the cops are coming!" Dino screams up at Amos.

When Amos cocks his head, Dino squeezes out from under him. He races to his sleek red Corvette parked at the nearby curb and with tires burning rubber, speeds away.

Amos finally realizes what is about to happen when he hears the approaching sirens getting louder. He runs down the street to his car on the corner and jumps in. He ducks down just as several police cars and a paddy wagon arrive. The police rush inside the strip joint.

How Matthew has ended up with the black stripper draped around him on top of a broken table he's not quite sure, and he is embarrassed. "Oh, I'm sorry . . ."

he pleads while struggling to free her legs from around his shoulders and head.

A policeman lends a helping hand and untangles them with an amused look. "Come on, you two . . ." He takes them by their arms and leads them out of the strip joint.

Outside, they are being herded into the police wagon and Matthew turns and asks the stripper quietly, "Why did you help us?"

She gently reaches out and touches his innocent face. "Baby, my whole life I've known what it's like to be in a minority . . . just like you folks."

Amos, looking through the back window of his car, sees Matthew and the black stripper along with David and Joseph being herded into the police wagon.

Todd and Kevin are being escorted to a police car.

Kevin is furious. "Todd, what the hell are you hanging out with that low-life Dino and those no-good friends of his for? He's nothing but trouble!"

Angry and pissed, Todd glares at his twin brother, "I don't tell you how to run your life . . . don't tell me how to run mine!"

They're shoved into the police car.

Chapter 6

Inside the police station, Matthew, David, and Joseph, still in the English ill-fitting clothes that are now torn and rumpled from their encounter, are even more of a sorry-looking group.

Frightened and unsure of what is going to happen, they listen with heads hung to the gruff booking sergeant staring down at them from behind his desk.

"You're entitled to make one phone call to either your parents or an attorney."

Stunned and ashamed, the boys just stand there, giving no response.

"Well?" the impatient sergeant implores.

A deputy comes up and whispers in the sergeant's ear. The sergeant explodes incredulously. "They don't believe in attorneys? Well, I don't blame them for that! But no phones! Well, that's their problem . . . lock 'em up!"

The deputy shrugs to the boys as if he tried and starts to lead the forlorn young Amishmen toward their cells.

Amos' car races down the dark lane to the Ammann farmhouse. He jumps out and runs across to the extension where Ezra and Grandma Ammann live and knocks on the door.

Ezra comes to the door in his longjohns and is startled to see the breathless young man. "Amos! What are . . ."

Amos, in total panic, blurts out excitedly to Ezra, "Ezra, you come quick! Matthew is in Philadelphia! In jail with David Beiler and Joseph Miller!"

"*Philadelphia? Jail?* How did they . . ." The old man, stunned, tries to comprehend.

Amos, quickly cutting him off, continues, "Hurry, Ezra. I will explain on the way!"

"I will get my clothes!" Ezra turns and hurries back into the house.

Inside their bedroom, Hans and Rebecca have awakened to the muffled voices they hear outside. They get out of bed, go to the open window, and look down into the front yard. They see the old car in the lane with its motor running . . . then spot Amos hurrying back to it.

Hans is trying to wake up and asks Rebecca, "What's Amos doing here with a car?"

"Amos is not supposed to have a car!" Rebecca frowns.

Out of the living quarters, Ezra, still in his longjohns and carrying his clothes and shoes, runs across the lawn to the waiting car.

"Ezra! What's happening?" Hans calls down.

Ezra doesn't take time to explain but waves his hand up in acknowledgement. "I'll take care of it, Hans!"

A frightened Rebecca calls to him, "Take care of what?"

Struggling, Ezra gets into the car and slams the door. Amos' car races up the lane and disappears over the hill.

Hans and Rebecca, very concerned, see a confused Grandma Ammann in her nightgown come out of her door into the yard with her arms helplessly raised crying out, "What's happening? Where's Ezra?"

Dino's red convertible speeds down a deserted street that approaches a crummy, broken-down and abandoned warehouse and wharf. Towering above the area is a bridge that crosses the Delaware River to New Jersey.

Dino screeches to a stop in front of huge, closed security gates and impatiently honks.

The gates are cracked open and a heavily armed guard inside looks out and recognizes Dino. The gate opens.

Dino burns rubber as the Corvette darts forward to a ramp and a staircase leading to an upper door to the warehouse. The car screeches to a halt.

Shielded from the entrance and off an abutment of the warehouse, a couple of sleek powerboats are being loaded by a few men working very quickly in the background.

Dino flies out of his car, climbs the stairs, and enters the building.

The rundown offices are dimly lit while down below a couple of other workers are helping unload a fork-lift and handing crates to men on the wharf.

Dino enters and hurries to a nearby office. He snaps on a light, opens a desk drawer, and takes out a handgun and a switchblade knife. He puts them in his jacket and moves quickly back to the door.

Just as Dino emerges from the door, a form looms up next to him. "Jesus, Sal! You scared the hell out of me!" Dino jumps back from fright.

The tough-looking hood laughs. "Just checking. What the hell are you doing here at this hour, Dino?"

Dino is already moving to the outside door. "Just going to give some Amish fuckers the lesson of their lives! God, I hate them for blowing our operation in Lancaster."

Sal sighs. "It was a good cover renting that farm out in the boonies." Then, remembering. "By the way, Dino, tell Todd his shit is together for the schools."

Dino is already out the door.

Sal calls down the stairs to a departing Dino, " . . . and, oh yeah! Your dad wants to see you. Said it's something important!"

Dino waves, jumps in his car, and speeds toward the gates.

Inside the police station, Todd, trying to look angelic, and Kevin, looking concerned, are standing next to a deputy in front of the desk of the booking sergeant.

"Must be nice to have a dad that can just pick up a phone . . ." Then, disgusted, "You're released until the hearing."

Outside the police station, Ezra is walking Matthew up the dark street to Amos' car parked up the block next to an alley. Ezra sighs. "Joseph and David's parents will get them."

Matthew is totally distraught. "I'm sorry, Grandfather, for causing you such trouble."

Ezra shakes his head soulfully. "Trouble is what usually comes mixing with the English."

As Ezra and Matthew approach, Amos sees them and tries to start the car, but it won't turn over as he grinds away.

In the background, Todd and Kevin are coming down the police station steps and heading up the street.

Amos tries again without success and bangs his hands against the steering wheel. "Cow dung!" Frustrated, he gets out of the car and opens the hood.

Ezra gives a wry chuckle as they near. "Nothing as reliable as real horsepower . . . yah, Amos?"

Amos, at that moment, doesn't appreciate Ezra's humor and disgusted looks up from the hood after adjusting something. He gets back in the car and tries to start it again without success.

Just then, Todd and Kevin slow down as they're passing on the sidewalk.

Kevin remarks to Amos, "Sounds like your carburetor is flooded."

"Don't help those Amish fuckheads . . . !" Todd barks bitterly.

Amos, angry at his car, opens the door and begins getting out.

Todd takes it as a threat and starts toward him.

Just at that second, Dino's Corvette comes down the street and turns into the alley, screeching to a halt. Dino jumps out, adding to the confusion.

"Here, use this!" Dino reaches into his pocket and throws the switchblade knife to Todd, who is moving in on Amos.

Everyone is stunned when Dino pulls out a gun.

Kevin, the nearest to Dino, flies through the air at him. "No, Dino! We've had enough trouble for one night."

It is mass confusion. Dino and Kevin struggle for the gun and Todd and Amos are entwined in a test of strength for the knife.

Ezra nods to Matthew, who then joins in the struggle to get the switchblade away from Todd.

Ezra then moves to help Kevin take the gun away from Dino. Their arms are locked and stretched in the air with their hands on the gun.

It's only when Ezra's two strong farm hands join in the fray that he is able to wrest the gun away from Dino, along with Kevin's help. With all the strength the old man can muster, Ezra tosses the gun as far as he can down the street toward the police station. Almost in the same movement, Ezra clutches his heart and staggers.

Kevin, now that Dino momentarily is no longer a threat with the gun, joins the fight to help Amos and Matthew get the knife away from his brother.

41

Dino looks down the street to decide whether to go get the gun or join the fracas but at the same time he sees a police car in that direction approaching the police station. He decides to get out while the getting is good and jumps back in his car, screeching down the alley and disappearing around the back.

In the main struggle for the knife, Amos gets tripped when Todd joins the fracas. Amos falls into Ezra, who is now in a state of shock and clutching his chest while having a seizure.

Amos realizes what's happening to the old man and grabs Ezra as he's sinking to the pavement.

Todd, Matthew, and Kevin now trip over the body of Ezra and fall to the ground, locked in a life or death struggle with the knife. Suddenly, the struggle seems to be over as blood begins running out from under the entwined bodies on the ground.

Inside the police car the officers, looking up the street, react when they see the melee. Instantly they turn on the speed, flashing lights, and siren as they approach.

The officers jump out with guns drawn to an eerie silence of death.

Chapter 7

Inside a jail cell, Matthew, moaning, is pacing like a caged animal. He moves from the cell door to a barred window . . . then to a bare wire cot and back again to the cell door. Exhausted and devastated, he finally sinks down onto the cot and sits there in a state of shock.

Matthew begins to rock back and forth with his head down and his hands together in his lap. He seems comatose and keeps repeating the same words like a mantra. "Oh, God, forgive me! . . . Oh, God, forgive me! Please forgive me!"

The night lights line the driveway of a lovely English field stone home on the outskirts of Philadelphia's

Main Line. Obviously, this is not a home purchased with the salary of the Philadelphia chief of police.

Inside the living room, Royer, aged and handsome in spite of the added responsibilities of his job and ready-made family, is fixing a drink at the bar.

"Sure you won't have a nightcap?" He looks over to his wife who is on the couch reading.

Katherine is elegant in looks and stature. Dark hair frames her beautiful oval face and her eyes loom large and brown, with long lashes set against a flawless complexion. She is regal in every sense of the word. From the ambiance of her home and surroundings, it is obvious she is a Philadelphia socialite.

"No thanks, Jim, but enjoy . . . it's a little late for me."

They react to car doors slamming out front. Royer crosses over to the front door as it opens and Alex, Royer's stepdaughter, enters.

"Hi you guys . . ."

She's a vital young version of Katherine, lovely, elegant, and beautiful in her own right. Long blonde hair falls softly around her face and down her back, with sapphire blue eyes framed by dark lashes. It is obvious she has inherited the coloring of her Scandinavian born father. Her mischievous smile lights up a room when she enters and it is apparent she is well sought after by the opposite sex.

A very prim and somewhat foppish looking young man enters behind her. It is easy to see that he is from a well-to-do family and somewhat spoiled.

Alex gives Royer a kiss on the cheek and the young man, obviously playing up to Royer to impress him, extends his hand at the door. "As promised, Mr. Royer, not one minute past twelve."

Royer responds in a strong, fatherly manner, "Good boy, Harold."

Harold, smiling, turns to Katherine. "Good night, Mrs. Royer."

Katherine nods. "Good night, Harold."

As Harold leaves, Alex crosses the room and enters the kitchen. "I need a glass of milk. Be right back."

Katherine looks up at Royer and somewhat hesitatingly asks a question that has been on her mind the past few months. "Have you given any more thought about running for mayor, Jim? You've done such an outstanding job as police chief, you'd . . ."

Royer, slightly perturbed, answers quickly, "I thought we had that all settled." He pokes the ice cubes in his glass with his fingers. This is obviously a subject he doesn't want to pursue.

Katherine, not to be put off, continues to push. "Well, it's just . . . I talked with Dad today and he said he would finance a run."

"Katherine, you knew what I was when you married me . . . I'm happy . . ."

He takes a frustrated sip of his drink then adds, "With what I am doing right now."

Alex has returned with her milk and overheard her stepdad. "Oh, Mother, can't you just let people be?"

She crosses over and gives Royer an affectionate hug. "Night, big guy."

She turns, gives her mother a peck on the cheek, and crosses over to the stairs.

"Night, Mom . . . I love you both."

The phone rings and Royer moves to answer it. He hears Darren, his assistant, on the other end.

"Chief, sorry to bother you at home this late, but we have an Amish kid in jail booked for the murder of Admiral Sprague's son, Kevin, an Annapolis midshipman. The Amish boy is in a state of shock and practically comatose. You, being ex-Amish, I thought. . . ."

"What's his name?" Royer asks.

"Matthew Ammann," Darren answers.

"*MATTHEW AMMANN!*" Royer's reaction startles Katherine, who puts down her book.

Darren's voice continues. "Oh, yes, I forgot. His grandfather was involved and he's dead, too."

Stunned, Royer moves the phone away from his ear. "I'll be right there!"

Now curious, Katherine, who has been listening to the one-sided conversation, asks after he has hung up the phone, "Ammann . . . isn't that the name of that Amish family where . . ."

As a raw nerve snaps, he responds, "Yes, Katherine!"

Royer is obviously struggling with deep inner emotions. With a devastating sigh, he crosses the room to her and quietly adds, "Life never is what it appears to be . . . is it?"

Royer gives her a kiss on the cheek. "Katherine, I'm sorry, I've got to go."

Katherine, affectionately holding his hand and looking up at him with concern, pleads, "Couldn't Darren go for you . . . ? It's late."

Royer gestures a wave good-bye and quickly closes the door behind him.

In the semi-darkness, Katherine sits a moment with her own thoughts of how this wonderful, simple, yet complex man entered her life . . . and how everyone's life is of their own making.

Then it flashes through her mind how much of a mess she had made in her youth as a wild and rebellious debutante. How she had defied her father at every turn . . . even to not listening to his warning about running off and marrying a social climbing gold digger that her father detested.

Katherine's painful memory reflects on her face when she recalls his warning: "He has not one ounce of ambition and he has no guts! Let's face it . . . he's just marrying you for your money!"

Katherine sighs and remembers screaming at her father, "You should talk about ambition! You haven't worked a day in your life! Why, if it hadn't been for Great-Grandfather's munitions and World Wars I and II, you wouldn't have a cent!"

Katherine's face flushes at the thought, and inwardly she reflects, "If I had only known what great deeds and accomplishments Dad had already quietly done and was doing with the family fortune for the betterment of the underprivileged around the world."

To this day her heart sinks with the embarrassment of being so young, spoiled, and stupid.

She thinks about how, over the years, she has grown to love and adore her father for all the real values he brought into her life. After all, it was he who brought Royer into hers.

And then a warm, loving smile crosses her face and she looks at a picture of Alex next to her in the shadows. "She was the only good thing to come out of that marriage."

She thinks of how much Royer loves Alex and what a good father image he is, instead of Alex's real father who last was heard of dying of some social disease on a South Pacific island somewhere.

Katherine sighs, gets up, and crosses over to the entry hall. Suddenly Shakespeare's words flash through her mind: "Oh, what a tangled web we weave."

Once again she looks at the closed front door, turns off the other light, and silently climbs the stairs.

Again her thoughts turn to Royer and his telling her that when he was a young man he was not only shunned by the Amish but by his own mother and father as well. She always wondered why . . . and he never told her.

She reaches the top of the stairs, turns off the upper hall light, and enters their bedroom.

Darren, at police headquarters, is filling Royer in with details. Swiftly, they move through the halls of the police station to the jail section.

"It appears that Kevin Sprague's twin brother, Todd, was also involved."

"How?" Royer asks as they turn a corner in the cell-block.

Darren continues explaining as they walk. "It appears that Matthew went berserk when his grandfather was killed, and in a fit of rage he stabbed Kevin through the heart . . ."

"Jesus, what a tragedy," sighs Royer with a deep breath.

They arrive at Matthew's cell and a deputy starts to open the door.

Royer looks in and sees Matthew still sitting on the cot, almost doubled over in a fetal position. He quietly enters the cell and looks down at him.

"Matthew, I'm Police Chief Royer."

Slowly responding, Matthew looks up and for the first time breaks down and sobs. "I should have known better for us not to come . . . come into town. We don't belong among the English!"

Royer sits down on the cot next to Matthew and can't help but put one arm around the distraught Amish lad. "It's all right, Matthew, we'll get to the bottom of all this."

Matthew looks up at Royer, pleading, "If it weren't for me, Grandfather would still be alive. The Navy man would . . ." Matthew can't continue, as his throat constricts and tears of remorse stream down his face.

"What have I done . . . what have I done?"

Royer tries to comfort him. "You can't be responsible for the whole world, Matthew. Don't be so hard on yourself . . . we'll sort it all out, I promise you."

Royer stands up to go. Then remembering, he asks Matthew, "Do your parents know?"

Matthew, devastated at the very thought, drops his head onto his chest and can barely shake his head no.

Royer picks up Matthew's head in one hand and makes him look at him. "Until I get a lawyer for you, promise me you won't talk with anyone. Matthew . . . you understand?"

Again Royer commands in a firm voice, "Do you understand?"

Matthew nods as Royer quickly leaves the cell and calls back, "Remember, Matthew . . . no one!"

Chapter 8

The early morning mist rests on the neatly defined colorful patchwork of fields that stretch before him as Royer's car comes over the hill and down the lane toward the Ammann farm.

A dichotomy and myriad of thoughts race through his mind. Especially one Pennsylvania Dutch statement he heard as a little boy and which keeps coming back to him over and over again . . . "Undt too late smart!"

Not comprehending in the slightest, he remembers saying to his very stern father who was a Deacon in the Amish church and his devoutly religious mother, "What a dumb thing to say!"

Then his own disappointment when they didn't agree with him. "When you get older, you'll understand, James Royer," they replied without any further explanation.

He then recalls how smart and wise he thought he was when he wanted to get away from the Amish simple life, the repetition, the discipline, the inhibiting social control with its conformity of stifling sameness, dress, buggies, only an eighth-grade education, being told what to think and what not to think, and on and on.

Back flash! "Undt too late smart!"

He thinks about the choices he made then that have affected his whole being . . . choices that were choking his very soul.

He remembers the wonderful feeling of liberation and growth he experienced after making what he felt was the "right and worldly" decision to leave the Amish faith not long after taking his sacred lifelong vows of commitment.

Then shortly afterward, the reality and bitterness of being shunned by the whole community and his life-long friends, as well as suddenly losing the only security he'd ever known . . . his family.

How he felt being treated like a piece of dirt and the hurt of not even being welcomed or allowed in his own home by his God-fearing parents. Yet feeling in his soul that his mother's heart was breaking, knowing she'd never be able to hold or touch her son again.

He thinks about Katherine. How in his own way he loved her, but was it real . . . *was he true to himself?*

Then those words brought back the excitement and

freedom of seeing his first play and hearing Shakespeare's words for the first time from the stage: "To thine own self be true." And vowing never to break that vow to himself.

How naïve, he thought.

"Undt too late smart!" flashes through his mind once again.

Royer's reverie snaps when he pulls up in front of the very pristine Amish farmhouse, jolting him back to the unpleasant task ahead.

Unconsciously he groans and turns off the motor.

Getting out of the car he wonders why he has such a haunting affinity for this Amish lad sitting back in that Philadelphia jail cell. Perhaps it is because Matthew reminds him so much of himself at that age.

Upon hearing a car's motor being turned off, Rebecca and Hans open the front door and see a man getting out on the far side and start walking toward them.

Panicked at not knowing what happened to Matthew and Ezra, Rebecca runs toward the visitor with a very concerned Hans following her.

Rebecca suddenly stops, stunned when she recognizes James Royer. Her face flushes beneath the bonnet and her heart is pounding even faster as she stares at Royer, whom she hasn't seen in eighteen years.

Royer can't move. His head throbs with filled thoughts of "What ifs?"

They look at one another, each afraid to speak.

Royer breaks the silence. "The years have been kind to you, Rebecca."

"You, too, James Royer."

Hans comes up behind his wife and slips his arm gently around her.

"Hans." Royer acknowledges him.

Hans just nods his head.

Rebecca, finally realizing, then almost frantic, cries out, "It's Matthew! You're here about Matthew! Where's Ezra?"

Royer starts to lead Rebecca toward the pond. Hans follows next to her.

In their nightgowns at the front door of the farm-house, a sleepy group of children, Mary, Jacob, and Elizabeth, stagger out onto the porch. They observe Jim Royer talking and walking with their mother and father down near the pond, then see Rebecca's legs go practically out from under her as Royer grabs her, lending his support.

"Oh no! Oh no! Oh God, no!" she screams.

Frightened, the children start to run to their parents as their mother starts to uncontrollably sob. Hans gently takes Rebecca out of Royer's arms.

"I promise you both, I'll get Matthew the best lawyer in Pennsylvania," Royer in a reassuring voice tells them.

"We Amish do not resort to lawyers or courts of law," Hans, devastated and heartsick, moans.

"You have to, Hans!" Royer pleads.

Hans emphatically responds to Royer. "*No!* Absolutely No! It's not our way . . ." Then, remembering, "*You* . . . of all people should know that, James Royer."

Pleadingly, Royer looks at Rebecca.

Rebecca, torn apart by the news of the death of her father and her son in jail, tries to pull herself together when she sees her children racing toward her, frightened and wondering what's happened.

Royer looks at them and their innocent beauty. The "what might have been" sinks in.

The children cling to their parents as they look at the stranger who made their mother cry.

Rebecca breaks the silence. "Children, this is James Royer . . . James Royer, these are our children, Elizabeth, Mary, and Jacob."

Frightened, the children nod and stare up at Royer.

"They're beautiful," Royer says with a gentle touch to Mary's head in soft acknowledgement.

Uncomfortable and not wanting to talk further in front of them, Rebecca quietly points to the farmhouse. "Go back inside and get dressed. It's time for your chores."

Reluctantly and silently, still not knowing what has happened, they know enough to obey without questioning their parents, as all good Amish children learn from birth.

Royer starts to move back toward his car with

Rebecca and Hans following. "I'll get bail set for Matthew," Royer asserts.

Rebecca looks confused. "Bail?"

Hans is now torn, looking at his distraught wife. Then, turning to Royer, he reluctantly gives in. "I can't do in your world, James Royer, what you can do to help Matthew . . ." Then resigned, "So do what you must."

Rebecca gratefully touches Hans' arm.

Royer, thinking out loud, turns to Rebecca. "Rebecca, if you could go back to Philadelphia with me, you could bring Matthew back. In the meantime, I'll make arrangements for Ezra to be sent home."

Rebecca turns hopefully to Hans. "Is that permissible, Hans?"

Hans answers reassuringly to his wife. "I'll take care of the children and try to tell them gently what has happened." He nods toward Ezra's front door. "And I'll try and explain to Grandma Ammann."

By now, Grandma Ammann has come out on her front porch to see what all the commotion is about.

Rebecca gratefully looks at her husband and tenderly hugs him. "Thank you, Hans."

She turns and gets in Royer's car. Nodding to Hans, Royer gets in and closes the door. The car starts and begins to slowly pull away.

Hans, with mixed emotions, watches Royer's car with his wife inside disappear over the hill.

Chapter 9

News spreads very rapidly in an Amish community, in spite of the fact that there are no telephones, fax machines, or e-mail.

Outside Zimmerman's Grocery Store, in the town of Intercourse, which is the center of the Pennsylvania Dutch country, there is an unusual number of Amish men and women in excited early morning gossip.

It is usually later in the day when the town is filled with gawking tourists anxious to see for themselves these strange and fascinating people who look, act, and live as if they took a step back in time to another century, country, and society.

A group of older Amish men are listening to a rotund farmer conspiratorially whispering. ". . . and Matthew's in jail!"

There is a gasp among the men as he continues.

"Joseph's parents said that he told them it started at a 'Girlie' show in Philadelphia."

"Girlie Show?"

"Philadelphia?"

Various shocked reactions spread with the farmer secretly enjoying holding court. "Yah, and the King boy said when his car wouldn't start . . ."

"Amos has a *car*?" blurts out an old fossil next to him.

"Yah, that's how they got to Philadelphia."

Nearby, a group of Amish women are even more deeply intrigued. With their bonnets practically touching, they are eagerly listening to Mrs. Stoltzfus expound to her captive audience, "Beiler's boy told them he heard Ezra had a heart attack when . . ."

The short, pudgy woman next to Mrs. Stoltzfus interrupts in indignation and huffs, "What was that old coot doing at a . . ."

Suddenly there's a hush over the entire area in front of the store when Royer's car pulls up. There is a unanimous nodding of heads toward the car, as if pointing to something. They see Rebecca in the front seat listening to a man saying something to her as he gets out of the car. "Rebecca, my cell phone just died and I've got to call my office. So much for modern technology!" Frustrated, he tosses it in the back seat and goes to the pay phone on the porch of the store. He drops in some coins and dials.

There are awkward glances and buzzing and the

rotund farmer reacts in surprise when he stares at the phone booth. "Isn't that *James Royer*?"

"What's Rebecca doing with that shunned *Amishman*? She shouldn't . . ." the old fossil protests.

Mrs. Stoltzfus, lowering her voice, adds, "I wonder if Hans even knows . . ."

The pudgy woman looking at Rebecca chimes in, "There's no doubt . . . she never told him . . ."

Inside the car, Rebecca sits nervously when she sees her Amish friends staring at her. Near the breaking point, she tries to keep her composure and stares straight ahead, determined not to make eye contact with anyone.

At the open phone booth and in a rising, agitated voice, Royer shouts into the receiver, "What do you mean, no bail!?"

Royer is listening to Darren's voice on the other end of the line.

"Admiral Sprague's been putting political pressure on everyone for no bail. He says he's going to prosecute Matthew to the full extent for what he did to his son."

Royer takes a couple of deep breaths and looks back at Rebecca in his car. "Well, keep on trying . . . I'm coming right in!"

Rebecca, her throat now constricting, sees the older Amish woman, Mrs. Stoltzfus, waddle over to her side of the car and peer inside. "I'm sorry to hear, Rebecca, about your father. Ezra was a good man."

Trying to hold back the tears, Rebecca answers softly, "Thank you Mrs. Stoltzfus."

Mrs. Stoltzfus continues, "And I'm sorry with Matthew things have come to such a tragic . . ." then adding conspiratorially, "situation. I'll be *praying* for *all* of you." She meaningfully nods toward Royer, who is approaching the car, then turns and waddles quickly away.

Rebecca can only nod. She is somewhat relieved when Royer climbs into the car and, disgusted, slams the door. He backs the car up, then roars off down the street with the Amish men and women staring in shocked disbelief at the disappearing car.

At the pond in front of the Ammann farm, Hans is sitting among the wildflowers with Elizabeth, Jacob, and Mary.

Jacob is disturbed and frowning. "You mean . . ." obviously not understanding his father's words, "I'll never see Grandpa Ammann again?"

Hans struggles to answer his son. "No, Jacob. You'll never see him again in this world . . . but you will see him in the life beyond."

"You mean in Heaven?" Mary asks.

"Yes, Mary. That's the divine order of things." Hans

gently touches her shoulder. "We will all see him someday."

Elizabeth asks anxiously, "We *really will* see Matthew again, no?"

A few claps of thunder are heard in the distance. Hans takes a deep sigh and looks up the empty road at the gathering storm clouds. "Yes, Elizabeth, that's where your mother has gone . . . to fetch Matthew with Mr. Royer."

Chapter 10

Royer's car drives down the wet highway with rain pelting the windshield. The wipers, with their hypnotic sound, make the interior seem even more confining.

Rebecca and Royer, alone with their thoughts and afraid to look at one another, suffer the agony of their silence. Finally, they allow themselves a glance.

Royer immediately turns back and stares ahead. She, too, turns and looks out the side window.

He finally speaks. "Maybe if I had stayed . . . maybe all this wouldn't have happened."

Rebecca, still looking out the side window at the countryside getting washed with rain, replies softy, "We both know *now*, as sure as we both knew *then*, it could never be."

She starts to turn to look at Royer but can't.

Then, after a long silence, she continues. "But I still

feel your . . ." She's too emotional to go on, and her thoughts drift back to . . .

. . . that magnificent cloudy day in the bloom of her youth. She is driving a horse-drawn wagon full of hay down a lane surrounded on one side by an eight-foot high cornfield and a tree-lined creek on the other.

Royer's young face peers out from behind a row of corn stalks, watching in mischievous anticipation as Rebecca approaches. He is vigorous and handsome in his Amish straw hat and work clothes.

Royer jumps out into the lane in front of the horse and wagon and playfully shouts with his arms raised, *"Surprise!"*

The horse bolts to a stop with his front rearing hooves practically in Royer's face.

Rebecca struggles with the reins to calm the horse and chides, "James Royer, you know you shouldn't be here!" She looks around worriedly. "I don't want anyone to see us in our secret lane."

Royer, with youthful agility, bounds up onto the open wagon seat next to her and blurts out, "I couldn't wait, Rebecca, until Saturday night!"

He takes her hands in his and they become entwined together in the reins. He rushes on, "I couldn't stand it another minute . . . you're so beautiful!"

Rebecca, who is now blushing with the glow of young love, tries to raise her hand to her face and bonnet, but can't because of their entwined hands. "Go on with ya' and your sweet talk!"

With an uncontrollable urge to touch her, he can't untangle the reins fast enough. "I just had to see you . . . I just . . ."

They eagerly embrace and kiss tenderly, then passionately, then vigorously as they lose their balance and fall backward into the bed of the hay wagon. Laughing, they playfully and gently throw hay at one another. James takes Rebecca in his arms and they lay side by side.

"Have you thought any more about our getting married outside the Amish church?" James asks.

Rebecca is suddenly sad, like it's an old wound. "You know we can't do that . . . we'd be shunned and . . ."

In frustrated agony, he pleads once again to her, "Rebecca, there's a whole *great big world* out there." Then he eagerly adds, " . . . and we can become a *part of it!*"

Proudly, Rebecca chides, "We Amish have not changed 'our world' *or* 'our ways' in over three hundred years and have gotten along very well, thank you, James Royer!"

Excitedly, Royer raises up on his elbows. "Rebecca,

you just said it all . . . we haven't changed." He sighs. "And a society that stops continuing to grow becomes like a dinosaur . . . extinct by outliving its usefulness. I read . . . ."

Rebecca playfully reaches up and gently puts her hand over his mouth. "You are becoming *too worldly* and reading *too many books.* There is only one book you should spend more time on, James Royer, and that's the Bible, and it says in 1 Corinthians 3:19: 'The wisdom of this world is foolishness with God.'"

Her hand slides off his mouth and her fingers quiver as they touch his lips, then chin, ear, and neck. Her arm suddenly goes hungrily around him.

Royer, his whole body trembling, rolls over on top of Rebecca and holds her tightly. He whispers softly, "I just want to share everything with you . . ."

He kisses her deeply and passionately and begins to make love to her.

He whispers, "All I know is that I can't picture my world without you . . . Oh, Rebecca, I love you so."

In the passion of the moment, they're not even aware of the raindrops beginning to shower down on them in the wagon. The reinless horse slowly wanders down the lane as the heavens open up and it begins to pour.

Royer is staring straight ahead at the rain on the highway in front of him. The silence is unbearable, with Rebecca still watching the beads of water run down her side window.

Royer, almost reverently, finally breaks the moment. "There hasn't been a day I haven't thought of your body pressed next to mine."

A tear rolls down Rebecca's cheek and into her mouth.

"Maybe God is punishing us for not being true to our souls."

The silence builds and says it all.

Finally Royer, exhausted and wanting to explain the years of tender memories stored inside his heart and soul, gently speaks. "It's hard to live a lie . . ."

Still not able to look at one another, they allow their hands to touch on the seat as the car moves through the rain in the silence of their thoughts.

Chapter 11

A deputy is ushering Rebecca down through a dark cell corridor. They pass various prisoners who are making crude remarks and cat calls while rattling their cell doors.

Rebecca tries not to look or react to the terrible sight or smell of this ungodly place, but shudders inwardly at the horror of it all. She is more fearful than ever for Matthew's well being.

"Never saw a Salvation Army uniform like that."

A prisoner reaches through the bars for Rebecca. "Come here and just let me touch your tits!"

A dark figure, barely discernable in another cell, sees her Amish black dress and white prayer cap and shouts loudly, "What is she, a nun?"

"Hey, Babe, I haven't smelled pussy for weeks," someone calls out.

Another grabs his crotch and in a husky, guttural voice, adds, "Yeah, have I got something for you."

The deputy growls angrily, "Knock it off!"

Rebecca is having a hard time keeping her composure as she reacts to the zoo mentality and conditions. She turns to the deputy pleading, "This is no place for Matthew . . . he's not one of them!"

They finally arrive at Matthew's cell and the deputy unlocks it and says, "The chief said he'd be back and pick you up in a little while."

Matthew, still in his awkward-looking city clothes, is lying on the cot with one arm over his face and eyes. He reacts upon hearing Rebecca's voice and sits up immediately. Seeing his mother enter the cell, he flies off the cot and into her outstretched arms. Tears stream down their faces.

"Oh, Mother, I'm so sorry—I'm so sorry!"

Rebecca just rocks him in her arms and in her motherly soothing way tries to comfort him. She holds him close and keeps repeating, "Shh . . . Shh . . . I know in my heart you never meant to hurt anyone."

Matthew is inconsolable. "But Grandfather would . . ."

Rebecca puts her finger to his mouth and shushes him again. She continues to cradle him in her arms and comfort him as best she can.

Royer's chief of police office is the same as his no nonsense demeanor. He is pacing while listening to Darren, with a couple of other officers waiting impatiently for his attention.

Darren, frustrated, is bringing Royer up to speed on the latest information he has on the case. "Judge Marshall is reluctant to allow bail without Admiral Sprague's approval . . . he says if that kid gets out among the Amish on those farms, we'd never see him again."

"The hell we wouldn't!" snaps Royer. "That corrupt . . ." Royer bites his tongue. "Marshall wouldn't understand the meaning of an Amish handshake . . ."

Starting toward the door, Royer turns to the first officer and barks, "Brian, you take my two o'clock meeting on gun control with the Mayor."

And then turning to the other officer, he continues, "...and John, you cover me with that press conference on the Scorpion murder."

Shouting over his shoulder as he exits, he gives a final instruction. "And Darren—get hold of Roland Hazeltine. Tell him I want him to represent Matthew immediately. I'm on my way to see the judge."

With mixed reactions, they scatter hurriedly to comply.

Inside Matthew's cell, Rebecca and her son are now sitting on the cot. Matthew, devastated, looks at his mother and moans, "Now I'll never be able to take my vows. I'll be shunned forever . . . and now Father, because of me, will never become *bishop*!"

Frightened, he pleads, "Oh, Mother, what will become of me?"

"Hush, Matthew . . . We must not worry about that right now." Rebecca puts her hand on his cheek. "Matthew, it's times like these we must put our complete faith in God's hands. But there's also a saying in the Bible that 'God helps those who help themselves.'"

Just then they hear the deputy and Royer approach. The cell door is opened and Royer enters.

Rebecca gets off the cot and determinedly approaches Royer. "You heard my husband's wishes, and I've never gone against Hans since our wedding vows. Your laws are made by man...our laws are made by God."

But then in desperation, she pleads to Royer, "Do whatever it takes, James Royer, to get *our son* . . ."

Flustered, she quickly stammers, "I mean . . . my son out of here!"

In shock and disbelief, the enormity of her words sink in as Royer looks at Matthew . . . and then back to Rebecca.

Heartsick, vowing she would take it to her grave without Royer or Matthew ever knowing, Rebecca can't look in Royer's eyes. But suddenly, desperately realizing with head down, she turns her eyes toward Matthew and subtly shakes her head no to Royer ever so slightly.

Understanding, Royer then regains his composure and says slowly, "I'll get Matthew out of here as fast as I can. I've already taken the first step, Rebecca. I've contacted the best criminal lawyer there is, but right now, we've got to go."

Still stunned at the revelation, he turns and stares at Matthew.

Royer starts to leave the cell and turns back to reaffirm their prior understanding. " . . . Remember, Matthew, what I told you. Talk with no one!"

Realizing his mother is leaving, Matthew gets up and hugs her tightly.

Rebecca, drained of every emotion in her soul, fights back her tears and whispers to her son.

"Listen to . . . to everything James Royer tells you."

She quickly kisses Matthew on the forehead and leaves the cell with Royer.

Rebecca turns for one last look at Matthew and calls back. "Promise."

Matthew nods and sinks back onto the cot.

Chapter 12

Royer's car is traveling down an exclusive "Main Line" Philadelphia suburban road.

Momentarily forgetting her devastating problems, Rebecca, never in her life having seen anything outside her Amish community of Lancaster County, is enjoying the magnificent variety of trees and flowers, and the continually changing architecture of the different styled sumptuous homes and estates.

Her face reflects the awe of what she is thinking. "So many different kinds of buildings. So many different sizes and shapes." Rebecca, with a sigh, thinks about the sameness of the Amish community...all the houses, barns, silos, and fences with everything painted just plain white at home. Then her face flushes when she feels a twinge of envy and guilt as she wonders, "All this money . . ."

Royer studies her innocent, beautiful face and now the thought of Matthew comes to his mind. Concerned, his expression changes and he sadly asks, "Why didn't you tell me about Matthew?"

Rebecca turns and looks at the man she once knew in every vein and pore of her body, the man she believed, no doubt, she was going to spend the rest of her life with. Then she thinks about his question.

Quietly and with no remorse or bitterness she answers, "I never saw or heard from you again after you were shunned and left."

The car approaches the impressive entrance gates and driveway leading up to Katherine and Royer's home. Rebecca wonders why he is turning here, seeing the splendorous grounds and stately house at the end of the long driveway.

"Is this your house?" Rebecca turns and asks incredulously.

He thinks about her innocent question. "It's the home Katherine inherited." He sighs. "It's where I live."

Reflecting, Royer drives in silence a moment, then continues, "I guess it's no different than Hans living in your parent's house."

Rebecca thinks about this, then answers, "Yah . . . I guess."

The car pulls up in front of the sumptuous house and Royer shuts off the motor. He gets out and goes around to open the door and help Rebecca out of the car. Timid and apprehensive, she climbs the circular stairs to the front door with Royer.

Katherine is talking on the phone in the entry hall at the bottom of the stairs which lead into the living room. Her back is to the front door.

" . . . have you decided what you're wearing? I can't make up my mind . . ."

The front door opens and Royer and Rebecca enter behind her. Unaware of their presence, Katherine continues talking to her friend on the phone. "Maybe we should meet tomorrow for lunch and go shopping . . . I know it's hard to get Jim into a tux."

Rebecca feels awkward and ill at ease as she looks subtly at the luxurious surroundings. She feels uneasy listening to Katherine's conversation. Royer also is uncomfortable and shuts the door behind them. Katherine turns and is surprised to see her husband standing there with an Amish woman. "He just walked in, Cynthia. I've got to go—I'll call you later."

She hurriedly finishes the conversation and hangs up the phone.

Seeing the confused look on Katherine's face, Royer awkwardly tries to introduce Rebecca.

"Katherine, I'd like you to meet Rebecca Ammann, Matthew's mother."

Quickly composing herself, Katherine starts to extend her hand, but then hesitates, not sure if the Amish shake hands.

Rebecca realizes Katherine's plight and offers her

hand with a warm smile. "We Amish do shake hands
. . . and even with the English."

Katherine, instantly liking Rebecca, takes her hand
and smiles, too.

"It's just that I've never . . . I mean, I'm not really
acquainted with your customs."

Royer, anxious to explain to his wife why he brought
Rebecca to their home, quickly chimes in. "Katherine,
I couldn't leave Rebecca at headquarters and I need
to get to Judge Marshall's immediately. They're deny-
ing Matthew bail. Hope you don't . . ."

Katherine responds quickly. "Mind? Nonsense! You
did the right thing, Jim. Now go!"

Sighing with relief, Royer takes Rebecca's hands.
With deep concern, he reassuringly tells her, "I
promise you, Rebecca, somehow I'll get Matthew out
of there."

Rebecca, forgetting Katherine for a moment,
touches his arm as she looks at him. "I know you will,
James Royer."

Leaving, Royer turns to his wife and waves. "Thanks,
Katherine." He closes the door and heads toward his
car.

Katherine graciously goes over to Rebecca and gestures to her. "Please come in, Rebecca, and make
yourself at home."

Katherine ushers Rebecca into the living room and
Rebecca can't help but be awed when she stops and

looks at the furnishings, paintings, and tasteful surroundings. She has never seen anything so grand.

Embarrassed, she realizes Katherine is watching
her, and shyly says, "I'm sorry to stare Mrs. Royer. I
have never been in a home like this before."

Katherine, realizing Rebecca's discomfort, answers
gently, "Please call me Katherine, Rebecca."

Katherine then tries to ease the awkward situation
with a lighthearted comment. "I can't imagine . . . is it
true you have no electricity, appliances, telephones,
closets for clothes . . . ?"

Rebecca responds with relief to have something to
talk about. "Yes, it's true, Mrs.—I mean, Katherine.
Our ways haven't changed much in three hundred
years."

Rebecca then looks down and her hand subconsciously touches a piece of sculpture next to her on a
table. "It's against our religion to covet worldly pos-
sessions . . ."

Rebecca's voice breaks when her eye catches Jim
and Katherine's wedding picture next to the sculpture. She withdraws her hand and moves off trying to
collect her thoughts. "Ah . . . that's why most of our
houses, inside and out, look alike and why we dress
alike. We're not permitted vanity or to show any signs
of . . ." She stops, not wanting to offend Katherine and
then continues, " . . . we are to be equal in the eyes of
God."

Katherine laughs gently, takes Rebecca's arm, and leads her off. Amused with her own thoughts of what she has just heard, she smilingly tells Rebecca, "In the universe of 'one-upmanship' that I live in, I wouldn't last five seconds in your Amish world. Come, let me fix you a cup of tea."

Chapter 13

Through the windows of Admiral Sprague's office, the Philadelphia U.S. Navy Base on the Delaware River can be seen with boats passing in the background. The admiral's office is filled with Navy mementos from Annapolis, World War II, and the present day.

Behind his desk Admiral Sprague, an imposing man with gray hair, obviously is devastated at the loss of his son. He's holding a framed picture of Kevin in his Midshipman Plebe uniform. The admiral, deep in his thoughts, hears a timid knock and the voice of Todd. "Dad, can I talk with you?"

Admiral Sprague sighs and puts the picture back on his desk. "Come in, Todd."

Entering, Todd is obviously a completely different person than he was the night before. He feels awkward and ill at ease in his father's intimidating presence, and not knowing how to start the conversation, finally stammers, " . . . Dad, I know how proud you were of Kevin." Now struggling, he hesitates for words.

He's not so sure he should have started this, and by now groping for words, continues on. " . . . and how disappointed you were when I didn't make Annapolis too . . . but ah . . . about the other night with Kevin."

He's now at the breaking point. "I want to tell you . . ."

"Todd, do you think this is a good time for this discussion?" The Admiral takes a deep breath and sighs.

Todd, put off and disappointed, tries to continue. "It's just that . . ."

Over the intercom, the admiral's assistant's voice is heard. "Admiral, I'm sorry to interrupt, but Police Chief Royer is here to see you."

"Send him in." Admiral Sprague, heavy-hearted, gets up. "Todd, we'll pick this up at a later time."

Todd, disheartened, but also not anxious to meet the police chief, stands up and starts toward the door. "Yeah . . . sure, Dad."

At this moment, Royer enters and the admiral nods toward his son. "Chief Royer, my son Todd, Kevin's twin brother."

Royer extends his hand to Todd who barely shakes it, almost as if it were a red-hot poker. "I'm sorry about your brother, Todd . . ."

Royer moves on to shake the admiral's hand. " . . . and your son, Admiral. You must have been very proud of him."

Admiral Sprague shakes Royer's hand. "Yes, I am."

Suddenly realizing he has the wrong tense and with a tear in his voice, he corrects himself. "I mean . . ."

He then draws himself up and proudly continues. "He was chosen the most likely to make first admiral from his class, and he was first in academics in a class of fourteen hundred and ninety-eight!"

Todd has heard this all too many times before and is anxious to leave as he edges toward the door. Meanwhile, the admiral continues with almost a eulogy. "He was heading toward an outstanding military career and..."

Todd is now at the door and turns to speak to his father. "Dad, I've got to go . . ." He nods to Royer in acknowledgement. "Chief Royer . . ."

Royer calls out to Todd just as he reaches the door, "Oh, Todd, tomorrow at your convenience, would you please stop by police headquarters for a deposition? We need your help."

Todd, very uneasy at this point, responds. "Sure, Chief Royer."

Todd hurriedly exits and Royer turns back to Admiral Sprague.

Knowing how distraught the admiral is about the death of his son, he is anxious to get this over with. "Admiral, I won't take up a lot of your time, but I'd like you to call off the wolves and let the Ammann boy out on bail."

The admiral starts to protest, but Royer continues

on quickly. "I've been to the D.A. and to Judge Marshall . . . I know the pressure you've put on them and I know your concern."

The Admiral, tired and exhausted, sits down behind his desk, listening to Royer's explanation. "So I've worked out a compromise, if it's all right with you. He's to be released to me and remain in Philadelphia in my custody, except for the few hours when I take him to his grandfather's funeral."

Admiral Sprague is on the verge of cracking. His hands tremble as they touch the outer edge of Kevin's picture frame. Without looking up, he nods his approval to Royer.

Relieved, Royer heads for the door and turns. "Thank you, Admiral Sprague."

The admiral recovers and stands up behind his desk, and now very much the professional, addresses Royer with a parting comment. "Oh, by the way, Royer, I've implemented *'your plan'* and we'll be ready."

"That's good news, Admiral. We're *closing in* on our end and we'll let you know." Royer quickly exits and closes the door behind him.

Completely spent, Admiral Sprague looks down at the picture of Kevin, the pride and joy of his life. Then, almost silently, whispers to himself, "How can two brothers be so different . . . ?"

Chapter 14

The Pennsylvania State Penitentiary is a foreboding fortress and seems extremely ominous in the overcast steel gray afternoon light. Dino's red Corvette drives in and parks in the visitor's parking lot.

Dino gets out of the Corvette and stares at the entrance looming in front of him. He takes a deep breath then starts toward the iron gates.

A tough guard is opening the cell door and calls in over the noise of the cellblock, "Come on . . . I haven't got all day . . . you've got a visitor."

A swarthy figure in prison blues gets off his cot,

exits the cell with the guard and starts down the confined walkway.

In the visitor's shakedown room, Dino is getting the full treatment. With his arms raised, a big, rough black female guard is giving him the once over with a metal detector. As she comes up the inside of one of his legs, she lets the antenna hit his crotch. Dino winces. She smiles, knowing full well what she did. "Sorry . . . okay . . . through there."

Dino wants to belt her, but goes to a door where another guard lets him into the visiting room.

Other visitors are seated and talking through a glass partition to the prisoners via phones.

Dino takes an open seat and nervously waits while looking at the guards stationed at each end of the room. He hears the door loudly clang on the prisoners' side and his eyes quickly dart in that direction. A guard from the cellblock is ushering a prisoner in.

Stopping for a second and framed in the door is mobster Angelo Bertolli, hardened even more by prison life. He has a mean scar from his ear to his chin and his face shows the mask of the violent criminal life he has led since his youth.

He sees his son and walks over to the seat opposite him. He picks up the two-way phone and waits for Dino to speak.

Dino, in a defiant tone, snaps, "Salvatore said you wanted to see me."

Bertolli, smiling for the guards' effect only, replies,

but his voice to Dino belies his looks. "So glad you made the effort, *son!*"

"Dad, don't start . . ."

Bertolli, continuing while smiling the whole time, says, "Don't start? Listen to me, and listen to me good. I'm only six months from getting out of this hell hole and after all these years I'm not going to have *you* blow it for me."

Then, looking at the guard, he snaps to Dino, "Smile, damn it!"

Dino makes a half-hearted effort to smile.

Bertolli continues, obviously seething inside, but controlling all outward expressions that might be picked up by the ever-present guards.

"They tell me you and that candy-assed Todd kid are doing some barn burning to get your kicks."

Dino can no longer contain his rage. "If it weren't for the *fucking* Amish, you wouldn't be here! I hate them!"

Bertolli, struggling to still smile, but all the while wanting to smack Dino a good one, replies in a low tone. "Christ, that's all I need is for that self-righteous Royer bastard to start sniffing around. When they threw me in here, they didn't even touch the tip of the iceberg. They only got one small operation . . . God, you're dumb!"

Bertolli's mouth now tightens and he forgets about smiling. In the same low tone, he continues to berate Dino. "Now I just got tipped off that Royer is looking for a friend of Todd's in connection with his brother's stabbing by that Ammann kid."

Dino is startled by his father's knowledge of the latest events. "I didn't think . . ."

Bertolli snaps back at his son. "Damn right, you didn't think!" He then takes a deep breath and realizes he's not smiling. He looks over at the guard at the end of the visitor's room, gives him a nod, and regains his forced smile. "God, it's too bad I didn't get that son of a bitch Royer when I had the chance."

Bertolli, with his free hand, pretends to rub his eyes with his fingers but his hand covers his mouth and under his breath hisses, "When you get back in town, tell Salvatore to close down immediately! We've got to move the operation to Jersey. Smile . . . *You got it?*"

Dino, smiling sarcastically, answers, "Yeah, Dad, I *GOT* it!"

Bertolli narrows his eyes and stares at Dino. Meaningfully, he slams down the phone and gets up.

A chill goes up Dino's spine as he puts down his phone and watches his father go to the door leading back to the cells. Bertolli stops for a moment and says something to the guard. Turning, he smiles and gives a wave to his son, who is exiting the visitor's door without looking back.

Chapter 15

Through the patio windows and doors in the den of the Royer home, the early evening shadows fall across the pool and elegant grounds.

On the coffee table in front of Katherine and Rebecca it is apparent, from the empty cups, that tea has long been over. Obviously nervous and ill at ease, Rebecca is listening to Katherine extol about Royer.

"Dad said he'd never seen anyone at the university ever have such a thirst for knowledge as Jim. Dad, being chairman of the board of trustees, couldn't believe the story that was brought to him about this young man from an Amish farm with practically no education at all. He was living in the ghetto slums without any money, except for various odd jobs he did as a carpenter . . . the only craft he knew . . . so he could get his high school diploma and go to college."

Proudly, Katherine reflects further. "I don't know how Jim did it. The university, classes, working, studying around the clock . . . and then graduating cum laude . . ."

Katherine notices Rebecca squirming slightly and restlessly moving her entwined fingers.

"Oh, but I guess you've heard all about this among the Amish."

Rebecca, lowering her eyes to her hands, softly answers, "No, we know nothing of this."

Seeing at least a sign of response from Rebecca, Katherine takes this as a sign of encouragement and to alleviate the awkward silence continues.

"Well Dad, through the family philanthropic endowments to the DuMont University and its School of Social Sciences, felt Jim would be perfect to go to work for them."

"I don't understand?" Rebecca inquires.

"When he found out, Jim felt God had put him in the ghetto for a reason, to see the lack of education, discipline, and disrespect for family values among the poor. Dad felt they shared a common dedication to making a difference. That's why he went to law school with a minor in social sciences. He wanted to dedicate his life to making a difference."

Rebecca is now a bit overwhelmed but intently listening. Confused and curious, she asks Katherine, "But what's that got to do with James Royer being chief of police?"

Katherine continues, happy to finally have something to talk about with Rebecca, knowing they have
very little in common otherwise. "Dad became Jim's
mentor and he immediately bonded to him. He was
attracted to his work ethics, honesty, and dedication
. . . especially his administrative abilities, which he
noticed while Jim was working for the DuMont
Charitable Trust Foundation."

Katherine gets a wry smile on her face and adds, "I
guess that's why Dad brought him home to me . . .
knowing I needed some of those values and ground-
ing."

She sighs, adding, "And little Alex needed some sta-
bility."

Rebecca shifts her body somewhat impatiently as
Katherine digresses.

Curiously she exclaims, "But James Royer hates
guns and violence!"

Katherine, now thinking about it, tries to further
explain. "That's exactly how Dad convinced Jim to
run for chief of police . . . because violence and cor-
ruption were out of control throughout the city, and
even the police force!"

Rebecca, still confused, again repeats, "I don't
understand."

"Well, with Dad's financial backing and political
support, combined with their common goals of solving Philadelphia's social problems, what better way
than to have a man in charge who would first think

out a non-violent, pacifist way of solving these problems? Jim *knew* in his heart he *could* make a difference in reducing crime and *could* give the police force a much better image through different kinds of actions, attitudes, and . . ."

Just then, they hear a car drive up in the back parking area. Relieved, Katherine ventures, "That must be Jim now."

Rebecca anxiously gets up when she hears the car door slam. The back door opens and an exuberant Alex enters, carrying her school satchel.

"Oh, it's you . . ." Katherine comments.

Alex, kidding her mother as she notices the Amish woman, says, "Well, thanks, Mother . . . that's some greeting."

She quickly crosses over to Rebecca and introduces herself. "I'm Alexandria, Mother's favorite daughter, seeing I'm her only child."

Rebecca, liking her immediately, shakes her hand warmly. "I'm Rebecca Ammann."

"Rebecca's waiting for Jim to bring her son here so she can take him home," Katherine explains.

Alex, now really looking at Rebecca, spontaneously adds, "You're beautiful."

Rebecca blushes, not used to flattery. She watches Alex hurry out of the room.

Alex calls over her shoulder as she leaves. "I've got to change, Mom, and get back . . . it's Monday night! It was nice meeting you, Mrs. Ammann."

She goes up the back stairs and heads toward her bedroom.

Katherine turns to Rebecca and volunteers, "She's pledging a sorority at Villanova University."

Rebecca, not knowing what she is talking about, just nods.

They hear the sound of two cars pulling up in front of the house. Katherine and Rebecca anxiously cross over to the entry hall just as Royer enters with Matthew.

Rebecca couldn't be more radiant as she takes Matthew into her arms, almost hugging his breath away. "Oh, thank you, thank you, James Royer. Now we can go home."

Royer appears concerned when he looks at Katherine, who by now is also relieved to get on with her life.

Struggling to find the right words, Royer looks at Rebecca and tries to explain the situation as kindly and gently as he can. "Rebecca, it's not quite that simple. The only way I could get Matthew released was to have him put in my custody and remain here in Philadelphia, except for going home for Ezra's funeral."

Rebecca is stunned. "You mean here . . . in your *house?*"

Looking for help, Royer turns to Katherine. "He could stay in the guest house over the garage . . . ?" Pleadingly, he adds, "It was the only way."

Katherine walks over to Matthew and extends her hand. "I'm Jim's wife, and you're welcome here, Matthew."

Matthew looks at Rebecca, who appears confused and concerned. Things are happening so fast.

Matthew finally finds his tongue. "Thank you, Mrs. Royer."

Turning, Royer addresses Rebecca. "Rebecca, my assistant Darren is going to drive you home. He's waiting outside."

Just then, Alex bounds down the stairs, looking especially attractive dressed for the sorority and fraternity night on campus. She stops on the stairs when she sees Matthew and the group.

Katherine extends her palm to introduce the two young people. "Matthew, this is our daughter, Alex."

Matthew looks up and his eyes and face reflect his astonishment at her beauty.

Katherine continues. "Alex, this is Matthew. He is going to be staying with us for awhile."

Alex bounds down the rest of the way and shakes Matthew's hand. "Great! We'll take good care of him, Mrs. Ammann."

She studies his clothes for a second with a quizzical look. "I didn't think the Amish dressed like *that*."

Embarrassed and suddenly self-conscious, Matthew awkwardly touches his ill-fitting clothes and quickly stammers, "These aren't my clothes. My clothes are . . ."

Rebecca feels his embarrassment and tries to offer a

solution. "I'll have Mr. Royer's assistant bring back your real clothes, Matthew."

Alex hurries out toward the kitchen. "Night everyone. I'm late."

Disappearing into the kitchen and family room area, they hear the back door slam and her car start.

Rebecca is now a raw nerve end and just stands in bewildered silence. Royer turns to her compassionately. "I know, Rebecca, this isn't going to be easy . . ."

His heart is pounding not being able to take her in his arms and cradle her.

Rebecca proudly pulls herself together and starts for the front door. Matthew follows her outside to the porch, along with Royer and Katherine. With the palm of her hand, Rebecca lifts Matthew's chin up and speaks to him. "It's better you are here, Matthew, than in that horrible jail . . ."

Turning to Royer, she continues. "You know, James Royer, how we Amish feel about mixing with the English . . ."

Frustrated and almost more than she can bear, she adds, "And *now* he's going to live in your house!"

Royer, trying to be light, volunteers, "It's not that bad, Rebecca."

Not understanding, she gives him a troubled look.

"Sorry, Rebecca, I was just trying to be funny."

Katherine, knowing all too well how a mother would feel in this situation, answers in a reassuring manner.

"I'll take care of Matthew, Rebecca, as if he were my own."

Now barely hanging on, Rebecca nods and starts down the stairs to the waiting car.

Matthew follows her, his face showing the pain at not being able to go home and the thought of what he has caused. It is almost more than he can endure.

At the bottom of the stairs, Rebecca looks back at the impressive home with Royer and Katherine standing on the porch. She turns and holds Matthew closely to her and speaks softly to him. "Remember, Matthew, the Amish teachings will always keep you in God's grace . . ."

"I will, Mother." He fights back his tears.

Rebecca, her heart at the breaking point, looks up once more at Royer. " . . . And resist the seduction of worldly goods and temptations of the outside world."

She turns and hurries to the car. Just before getting in she calls back to Matthew, "I don't want to lose you, Matthew."

Matthew's eyes water as he tries to reassure her. "You won't, Mother."

Then he quickly adds, " . . . and tell Father, Elizabeth, Mary, and Jacob to pray for me."

Deeply concerned, Royer watches Darren's car wind its way down the driveway, taking Rebecca back to her world and family that he can never be part of.

He watches Matthew wave good-bye to his mother,

knowing, too, his son will never know about him or be part of his world and family.

Inside the car, Rebecca looks back with tears rolling down her face. She sees her son, with his arm still waving getting smaller and smaller. In the background, Royer and Katherine are standing on the porch of their home as they watch Rebecca disappear down the road.

Chapter 16

Royer, Alex, Matthew, and Katherine are in the midst of breakfast in the kitchen-family room area. Matthew is back in his Amish clothes, but obviously uncomfortable. Katherine is pouring Royer some coffee and Alex's satchel is on the counter behind her.

"Thanks, Katherine," Royer nods as she finishes pouring.

"And where do you go to school, Matthew?" Alex asks.

Matthew squirms, searching for the right words. "Ah . . . I've been out of school four years."

Katherine is startled and asks, "Why, you're not that old to . . ."

Matthew continues, trying to explain as best he can. "We only go to Amish school through the eighth grade, Mrs. Royer . . . the Bible says in 1 Corinthians

3:19 that 'The wisdom of this world is foolishness with God.'"

Royer looks at Matthew and his thoughts drift to Rebecca saying the very same words to him in the hay wagon and how much Matthew reminds him of her.

Alex is fascinated with Matthew. His innocence seems to intrigue her and she continues to question him. "Well, what do they teach you that you can leave school so early?"

Matthew replies, now hoping his answer will end all the questions being asked him. "Besides the three 'r's, we're taught thoroughly before leaving school to live by example, to have respect for our elders and authority, to learn the Amish teachings of calmness of mind, conquest of selfishness, silence of the soul, and that we must have simple values and reside in the teachings of Christ . . ."

There is silence at the table. Matthew starts to worry, and hurriedly asks, "Did I say something wrong, yes?"

Royer reaches over and tousles Matthew's hair as he gets up from the table. "No, you didn't say anything wrong. After what's been happening in our schools, we'd be better off if we took a few lessons from the Amish."

Katherine gets up to clear the dishes. Smiling, she turns to speak to Matthew. "Matthew, talking with your mother yesterday made me ashamed to realize the most important appointments I have each week are for my hair and my nails."

Alex jumps up out of her seat and gives Matthew a peck on his cheek. "I'm anxious to spend more time with you, Matthew. You're adorable!"

Matthew blushes and doesn't know how to react to such a beautiful free spirit.

Alex grabs her satchel and busses Royer and Katherine. On her way out the back door and not waiting for an answer, her parting words are casually directed toward Katherine.

"Hope it's all right, Mom, I'm having some girls over to study this afternoon."

Royer also gives Katherine a kiss on the cheek and heads out. He stops and turns to Matthew. "Oh, Matthew, the attorney, Mr. Hazeltine, will be over to see you sometime today. Remember, talk to no one but him."

Matthew nods, understanding what Royer has said. "I promise, Mr. Royer."

Matthew gets up and starts to help Katherine clear the dishes from the table. Katherine, with a warm, surprised smile, gratefully acknowledges his assistance. "Why, thank you, Matthew."

Inside the Ammann barn, the light rays filter between the cracks of the barn sidings. The light from the open barn door at the far end silhouette Mary, Elizabeth, and Jacob playing hopscotch.

In the hay, Hans and Rebecca are on their knees tending a mare on the verge of giving birth to a foal. Hans, tender with his hands, rubs the mare and tries to soothe her. "It's not much longer."

Hans looks up at Rebecca, whose thoughts are elsewhere. Wistfully she asks Hans, "Why do some humans cloud the miracle of birth with so many rules and restrictions?"

Hans, with a deep sigh, looks meaningfully at Rebecca and profoundly responds as best he can. "Maybe that is why God made us humans instead of animals . . . to have a conscience."

Rebecca, reflecting for a moment, answers, "Yah, I guess so, Hans."

Worried, he studies his wife for a second, then continues on with a subject he has not been looking forward to sharing. "Rebecca, Bishop Anken and the Elders came to see me yesterday while you were gone. They are starting excommunication proceedings against Matthew."

In shocked disbelief, Rebecca blurts out, "Oh, no, Hans, they can't! Matthew has to take his vows."

"Yes . . . they can, Rebecca. The Bishop is concerned that Elizabeth, Mary, and Jacob will be led astray."

With a plea in her voice, Rebecca says, "But Matthew wouldn't . . ."

"They're adamant in their feelings. 'Violence begets violence' and 'Peace begets peace.' Matthew is . . ."

Suddenly Hans is interrupted when the mare lets go several piercing sounds of giving birth that echo through the barn. The children race across the interior and gather around the mare. They are wide-eyed as they watch the birth of the foal and the natural unfoldment of life with all its wonders.

Hans and Rebecca, now both assisting, also marvel at the experience and watch as the colt struggles to stand on its wobbly legs.

"Matthew, where's Matthew? He wanted to be here too!" Jacob questioningly calls out.

"Yes, Mother, when is Matthew coming home?" Elizabeth asks anxiously.

Mary ruefully adds, "I miss him."

Rebecca fights to keep back the tears and touches Mary's hair. "Me, too, Mary." Then, remembering. "For a while, he'll be here tomorrow for Grandfather's funeral."

Jacob looks up at his mother, as only a four-year old boy can, and asks, "Mother, what do you mean, 'for a while?'"

Rebecca is too choked up to answer and Hans has to come to her rescue. "It's time for your afternoon chores. Now go and we'll talk about it at dinner."

The children scamper off. Hans assists Rebecca to

her feet. Her eyes reflect her thanks as they walk toward the open barn doors.

Chapter 17

In front of the Royer home sits an expensive but sedate four-door Mercedes. Matthew is at the front door and the distinguished attorney, Roland Hazeltine, is starting down the steps. He turns and looks at Matthew, leaving him with one last parting statement. "Be assured, Matthew, we'll do everything possible."

Roland Hazeltine gets in his car and Matthew closes the door. He watches him drive off down the long driveway and through the gates. Sighing, he turns and heads back toward the house.

Stepping back into the entry hall, Matthew hears some girls giggling and a few splashes coming from the pool. He crosses to the French doors leading to the backyard and peers out.

Much to his astonishment, Matthew sees Alex and four of her sorority sisters in very skimpy, sexy bikinis soaking in the afternoon sun. Their books are in evidence next to the chaise lounges and tables.

His eyes reflect his awe and appreciation, but then change to the dreaded fear of being found a peeping Tom when he hears Alex call out, "Oh, Matthew, come out . . ."

Alex is looking exceptionally sexy while rubbing oil on her body.

The girls see Matthew looking through the glass doors, wide-eyed and in frozen fear.

Alex continues urging him. " . . . I want you to meet some friends of mine."

Matthew picks up his Amish black hat from a nearby table and sheepishly comes out to the pool.

Alex points. "Matthew, this is Debra, Joan, Annabelle, and Marilyn. Girls, this is Matthew."

Matthew in his Amish clothes and hat presents quite an unusual sight to these nearly nude girls.

"Join us, Matthew." Seductively, Joan wiggles her finger towards the pool.

"You're right, Alex, he is cute," Annabelle confirms.

"Hi, Matthew," Marilyn coos.

Marilyn, now getting out of the pool, eyes him up and down with appreciation. "You're the first Amishman I've ever met. I didn't know they were so handsome."

Marilyn, knowing full well what she is doing, bends over practically coming out of her top. She offers Matthew a chair next to her. He awkwardly accepts it, trying not to look at the fantastic exterior of her lungs. Instead of paying attention to the chair, Matthew practically misses it and almost tips over as he sits.

Joan now adds her two cents from the pool. "Alex has been telling us some of your quaint customs."

Debra agrees, but now with youthful curiosity asks, "Yeah, the thing that blows me away is how do the kids ever get together if they have such strict rules and regulations?"

Matthew takes off his hat and nervously turns it while he ponders the question, all the while not taking his eyes off Alex. She gets up from the lounge chair and gracefully slides into the pool.

Remembering he hadn't answered Debra's question, Matthew stammers, " . . . Ah . . . on Sunday evenings after dinner, we have singing."

Annabelle incredulously blurts out, *"Singing!?"*

Matthew, finding his tongue, volunteers, "Yah! Young people gather around a long table in the barn, boys on one side and girls on the other, and we sing hymns."

"And that's *IT!?*" Joan, in total astonishment, asks.

Matthew, now kind of enjoying for the first time in his life being the center of attention, continues. "Well, there is a time between selections for conversation." Then he adds quickly, "And at ten o'clock, when singing ends, there is an hour more of joking and visiting."

107

The girls are truly fascinated.

Joan winks to Annabelle in the pool and adds, "Boy, that must be a *blast!*"

In spite of all the attention from the other girls, Matthew has not been able to take his eyes off Alex. She has been sensing this and swims directly over to Matthew by the side of the pool. She raises herself on the edge. Looking directly into Matthew's eyes she asks, "How do they . . . ah . . . *'make it'* together?"

Matthew looks confused. "Make it . . . ? Oh, you mean *Bei-schlof!*"

Now it's Alex's turn to be confused. *"Bei-schlof?"*

Matthew tries to clarify. "Bundle!"

Alex, still confused, repeats, *"Bundle?"*

Pleased that Alex is showing him some attention, Matthew further confides. "That's when you are going 'steady' and every other Saturday night you go to her house after the 'old folks' go to bed and you take your flashlight and shine it on her window . . ."

The girls are now in rapt attention, not taking their eyes off Matthew as he speaks. "When she sees the light, she knows he's there and goes down to let him in."

Joan is intently listening to every word Matthew is uttering.

"Well, they go upstairs and spend time together with their clothes on, just getting to know one another."

"No shit . . . you're *kidding!?*" Debra, in disbelief, asks.

Matthew volunteers innocently. "Kidding? Why would I do that? In the old days, they would have a bundling board that they would put between them."

"Yeah, sure . . ." Joan adds, winking at Debra.

"As if that'd do any good!" Debra laughs as she looks at the other girls in disbelief.

Marilyn checks her watch and starts gathering up her things, making sure Matthew gets the full treatment of her visible charms.

"Oh my God, look at the time. We've got to split."

The girls get out of the pool and quickly gather their belongings. Debra shakes Matthew's hand longer than necessary, while giving him a seductive look. "Thanks for the class in Sex Education 101A."

Matthew, not understanding, asks, "Sex Education 101A?"

Marilyn pats him on the arm as she passes clarifying, "Just a joke, Matthew. Nice meeting you."

The girls go through the pool gate to the back parking area and Joan calls back, "Alex, see you mañana."

Alex waves to the girls as the car pulls away.

Looking at Alex, Matthew wonders why Sarah flashes through his mind. Is he comparing? Then he knows he is more than smitten by the charm, beauty, and excitement of this almost nude creature before him.

Alex is a vision of loveliness that a week ago he could never even have imagined in his wildest fantasies back in the sheltered Amish existence he lived on the farm.

Then his mother's last words flash through his mind and a worried frown crosses his face. " . . . and resist the seduction of worldly goods and temptations of the outside world."

Alex, too, is surprised at the deep feelings stirring within her as she studies Matthew's face.

She thinks to herself, "Is it just that my girlfriends find Matthew so cute and attractive, or the fact that he is so sweet, innocent, and gentle . . . much different from all the boys I've dated?"

They both notice the silence of their thoughts, then Alex asks, "Why the frown, Matthew?" She puts her finger to his furrowed brow.

The touch of her finger sends feelings through his body he has never experienced before.

Not wanting to reveal his mother's admonitions, he tries to cover by saying, "Ah, I was just wondering what 'man-a-ah-ana' meant?"

Alex lets her finger gently move down to his mouth and laughs, "Mañana . . . it means tomorrow."

Alex feels his mouth quiver under her finger as they now look into each other's eyes. She slowly lets her finger touch his lower lip, then down his chin. She speaks softly, almost whispering. "They really 'dig' you."

Matthew starts to form the word 'dig', but this time she quickly puts two fingers to his lips. "Don't even ask. It means *really* like!"

She moves her fingers slowly along the side of his face and inches closer. "Me, too, Matthew . . . have you ever *Bei-schlofed?*"

Matthew blushes. Embarrassed, he shakes his head no ever so slightly. His whole body is trembling and their two heads move even closer. Now Alex, in slow wonderment, says, "I bet you've never even kissed a girl?"

Matthew's eyes reveal the answer and now her body starts to quiver as she moves closer and their lips touch. Alex pulls back and says softly, "Try again, Matthew . . ."

He does, and this time they kiss for real.

Chapter 18

The Amish graveyard is hugging the crest of a knoll overlooking the pristine Amish farms nestled in the valley below.

On the horizon, the Amish buggies are parked, their horses like sentinels in single file on the road along the ridge. Other horses and buggies, along with the funeral wagon, are standing at attention inside the cemetery gates.

One incongruous car is parked nearby with a lone figure leaning against it. It is James Royer, observing the scene below of family and friends gathered around Ezra's open grave in the middle of the cemetery.

Grandma Ammann is sobbing, while Rebecca, herself grief-stricken, is trying to comfort her with one arm while holding Matthew close to her with the other. Elizabeth and Mary are clinging to Hans on one side and Jacob on the other. They are all looking at Bishop Anken, who looks meaningfully at each one of them as he speaks.

"God has given Ezra Ammann a full life, surrounded by the love and devotion of his wife, Emily, his daughter, Rebecca, and caring son-in-law, Hans. Ezra was also blessed with the good Lord's gift to all grandparents, the grandchildren . . . Jacob, Mary, and Elizabeth . . ."

Bishop Ammann has a hard time continuing as he scowls and finally, reluctantly adds, " . . . and . . . Matthew Ammann."

Bishop Anken's words are drifting up to Royer, who sadly thinks, Will it be ever thus, an outsider, always looking in? There is the woman I should be comforting . . . and there is my son, the only living legacy on this earth to carry on my genes, my blood, my name . . . and he'll never know.

Rebecca glances up the hill for a split second, seeing Royer alone and shunned forever from his roots. A thought quickly flashes through her mind. Maybe I'm equally responsible. Suddenly a feeling of betrayal that she never let him know about Matthew floods her whole being. Maybe I could have found him if I'd tried.

Then Royer's words to her in the car come back hauntingly. "It's hard to live a lie."

Rebecca is not hearing Bishop Anken's words as he drones on. She glances at Hans and thoughts keep pouring through her mind. How hard it has been, not letting Hans know the lie I've been living all these years. How it would hurt him to know that Matthew is not his son. Even the lie when Hans arrived from the Amish community in Ohio to visit his sister and fell in love with me. How convenient it was to marry him and let him think Matthew was born prematurely.

Rebecca looks at Mary, Elizabeth, and Jacob, clinging to Hans, and in her heart knows she has grown to love him for all the blessings he's bestowed on her.

But is it God's will or just the punishment of my sins that these feelings still rage through me when I think of James Royer?

Rebecca is jolted back to reality when Jacob's little hand tugs on her skirt. She lovingly reaches down and takes it in hers.

Bishop Anken is surveying the Amish mourners, including the anguished young faces of Amos, David, and Joseph, as they listen to him conclude: " . . . and his neighbors who shared his love of life. Ezra Ammann gave me, not too long ago, something he wanted to share with you at this moment. It is titled, 'I Am Not There.'"

He then takes a piece of folded paper from his pocket and begins reading the poem, first in German and then in English, with each line:

"Stehe nicht an meinem Grab und weine:
   Do not stand at my grave and weep."

115

"Ich bin nicht dort, ich schlafe nicht
I am not there, I do not sleep."

"Ich bin die tausend Winde die wehen
I am a thousand winds that blow."

(Rebecca and Grandma Ammann no longer can hold back their tears.)

"Ich bin der schmmernde Diamant im Schnee
"I am the diamond glints on snow."

"Ich bin der Sonnenschein an reifem Korn
I am the sunlight on ripened grain."

"Ich bin des Herbstes sanfter Regen
I am the gentle Autumn's rain."

(The pallbearers lift the coffin with the straps and a Deacon quickly removes the supporting crosspieces.)

"Wenn Du im Morgengrauen erwachst:
When you awaken in the morning's hush,"

"Ich bin der Aufwind der die Vogel
I am the swift uplifting rush"

"Ihre Runden ziehen lasst,
Of quiet birds in circled flight."

(Ezra's coffin is slowly lowered into the grave.)

"Ich bin der milde Stern mit seinem Licht in der Nacht
I am the soft star that shines at night."

"Stehe nicht an meinem Grab und weine
Do not stand at my grave and cry,"

"Ich bin nicht dort .... Ich bin nicht tot.
I am not there . . . I did not die."

116

The long straps are now slowly removed.

Uncontrollable tears stream down Matthew's face. Rebecca, in her grief, draws Matthew to her and rocks him in her arms.

Still very much alone with his thoughts, Royer sees Rebecca and Matthew, then the children with Hans, who's trying to console them.

He thinks of how grateful he is that God put Matthew in the good loving hands of Hans. It flashes through his mind that the wisdom of God, with His infinite power, brought Alex into his life for him to practically raise as his own daughter. A slight smile crosses his face as he thinks inwardly, He surely does work in mysterious ways.

The Amish gathering of mourners now starts to move toward their buggies. Hans begins to shepherd his family gently up the hill.

"Mother, does Matthew have to go with Mr. Royer?" Jacob pleads.

"I'm afraid so, Jacob." She sighs and looks up the hill towards Royer.

Jacob turns with confidence to Hans and asks, "You can make Mr. Royer change his mind, can't you, Father?"

Hard put to answer, Hans scoops Jacob up in his arms.

Matthew comes to Hans' rescue and kneels down next to Jacob. "It's all right, Jacob. It's not Mr. Royer's fault I can't stay."

Royer is ill at ease while receiving all kinds of suspicious looks from his life-long Amish friends and mourners as they pass and get into their buggies.

Hans and his family walk toward him. Royer extends both of his hands to Rebecca. "I'm so sorry about Ezra. I wish things were different, Rebecca . . . about everything."

Rebecca, not wanting to let go of his comforting hands but afraid to look into his eyes, forgets that he is a shunned Amishman and should not be touched. When she remembers, she quickly pulls her hands away and says to him, "Thank you for bringing Matthew. I know you'll do right by him, James Royer."

She turns to Matthew and hugs him one last time. "Matthew, remember to say your prayers, and know you are in all our prayers each night."

"I will, Mother," he solemnly promises.

As Rebecca releases him, Mary, Elizabeth, and Jacob cling to their brother with their good-byes.

Mary hugs him and is on the verge of tears. "I miss you already, Matthew."

"I will do your chores for you, Matthew, until you come home," Elizabeth promises.

Trying to be old beyond his years, Jacob bravely blurts out. "I do not know what you did, Matthew, but I know it was not bad." He then jumps into his big brother's arms and starts to cry.

"Thank you, Jacob."

Matthew reaches over his little brother's body and

with tears in his eyes, extends his hand to Hans, "I'm so sorry, Father. I've disgraced you and our family."

By now Jacob has slid out of Matthew's arms to the ground.

Royer, with his heart breaking, watches Hans, uncharacteristic of the Amish and especially in public, pull Matthew to him and hug him. "You have always been a good son, Matthew. I know God's grace is within you."

Hans releases him and Matthew quickly gets in the car.

Royer, filled with a lifetime of emotions, looks at Rebecca. He then nods to Hans. "I know your feelings, Hans, about lawyers, courts, and such, but in the English world, a man is innocent until proven guilty."

Royer gets in the car as the children wave at Matthew. He slowly drives among the jumble of horses and buggies in the road. The grief is etched on Matthew's face as he looks out the window on his side of the car.

As they slowly pass a buggy, Matthew sees Sarah look across at him. She shyly raises her hand, waves, and tries to smile. At that moment, her mother's hand comes into view and moves Sarah's arm down.

Matthew tries to hide his tears from the police chief.

Rebecca, Hans, and the children are getting into their buggy and at the same time watch Royer's car go down the hill and disappear into the Amish landscape.

Chapter 19

Outside the wharf and warehouse there is an unusual amount of night activity, even though the area is dark. Todd drives up in what he thinks is a *bitchin* looking wide-bodied, high-tired pickup truck. He parks next to the ramp.

They have to move aside as two rough thugs carry a crummy desk and load it onto a truck backed up to the loading dock.

In the background, three sleek powerboats are being loaded from the side of the warehouse leading to the Delaware River.

Dino and Todd are both observing the busy activity going on all around them. Dino is high with excitement and turns to Todd as they start up the steps. "Won't be long and we're history . . . but we're all set up-river on the Jersey side."

"I won't mind the drive, just as long as I stay in business," Todd laments.

They enter the warehouse and carefully look around.

The dimly lit offices are practically gutted and there is frantic activity of forklifts hauling containers to the wharf and boats. Dino and Todd head down toward Dino's office as Salvatore steps out of his office and follows them. "Oh, Dino . . . I had them put your personal shit in . . ."

They enter Dino's office and Sal continues talking " . . . those boxes there."

"Thanks, Sal."

Pointing to a cardboard container and three plastic bags filled with white powder, Sal turns to Todd and says, " . . . and Todd, that's your stuff over there."

Todd moves to the container and on the way, takes an envelope out from inside his jacket and hands it to Salvatore. "Thanks, Sal . . . here."

Salvatore opens it and fans the contents, silently counting in his head.

"It's all there!" Todd glares defiantly.

Sal, with a snide smile, tucks the envelope into his jacket and zips it up. Snickering, he adds, "You haven't short changed us yet . . ."

Salvatore heads back to his office and stops. He turns to Dino with one last thought that has been eating at him all day. "I still think your old man is making a mistake and it's a waste of time . . ." He shakes his head, waves, and enters his office, calling back as he trails out of sight, "But what the hell, it's his show."

Muttering under his breath, a bitter Dino can't hold back his frustration and mumbles to himself, *"Isn't everything?"*

Chapter 20

Katherine looks regal in her St. John sequined evening gown. Royer seems ill at ease in his tux. They are seated at a dining room table next to a window at Philadelphia's finest country club, overlooking a beautifully lit terrace and golf course.

The dimly lit crystal chandeliers add to the romantic ambiance as a five-piece combo is playing "Tenderly," with couples dancing and enjoying the sentimental number.

Katherine reaches across the table and takes Royer's hand. "Considering everything, I think we've done rather well, don't . . ."

Just then, a couple passes by their table. "My, my, what a surprise to see you two!" Charlene gushes.

"Must be a special occasion, Katherine, for you to get Jim into a monkey suit." Norman taps Royer's shoulders and tux.

Katherine laughs and extends her hand. "It is, Norman . . . our tenth anniversary!"

Royer, with a touch of sarcasm, adds, "And I remember, Norman, overhearing Charlene at our wedding saying it would never last."

Charlene and Norman are not sure how Royer means it. Norman waves to the maitre d' who is nearby. "Robaire, a bottle of Dom Perignon for the celebration, while it lasts . . ."

Robaire nods with a pained expression as Norman laughs at his own stupid joke and moves on. "Yes, Mr. Fairchild."

Charlene busses Katherine's cheek and with insipid insincerity adds a last parting comment. "Happy anniversary, Katherine, and you, too, Jim. I think it's wonderful."

Katherine responds halfheartedly, but ever so sweetly. "Thanks, Charlene."

Royer, trying to contain himself, takes a long swig of his drink and mutters to Katherine, "Jesus Christ, they deserve each other . . . what asses."

Then realizing what he has just said, he raises his eyes skyward apologetically. "Sorry!"

"I'm not sorry . . . they really are asses!" Katherine adds supportively.

She then tries to regain the mood and reaches across for her husband's hand. "Are you happy you married me?"

After a long pause with no response, Katherine

hopefully adds, "I am, because I really love you, Jim . . ."

Royer is having a hard time keeping focused and not having heard her, apologetically asks, "I'm sorry, Katherine . . . what did you say?"

Katherine sighs and turns his hand over in her palm. Tracing her finger along his heart line, she gently murmurs, "I said you seemed distracted and far away."

Obviously troubled, and as best he can, Royer responds, "I was thinking about Matthew. Rebecca told me before the funeral that the Amish elders are going to shun him. God knows . . . of all people, I know what that does to a mother . . . let alone what it will do to Matthew for the rest of his life."

Katherine is struggling with her thoughts and inwardly wonders why her husband appears to be so protective of Rebecca. "Jim, you seem so overly caring and considerate toward Rebecca," she finally says.

Royer reacts somewhat defensively.

Opening up the floodgates of his pent up emotions after all these years, Royer takes Katherine's hands in his and begins to explain. "From the time Rebecca and I were little kids, we pretended that someday we would be married. Katherine, I practically left Rebecca at the altar after taking my sacred vows to never leave the Amish church.

"I thought that I could give up my passion for knowledge, my growing resentment toward my Amish heritage, being a conscientious objector, never being able to pledge allegiance to my flag, the pressure to conform to the majority way of life with their stifling righteousness, their fear of growth, the thought of being a farmer and knowing that's all Rebecca would ever want me to be, or expected me to be . . . and *I knew* she could not change, and *would* not change, and I would not *want* her to change."

Royer takes a deep breath and looks almost pleadingly into Katherine's eyes. "I knew all this and thought I could handle it, and that's when I took my vows to my church and asked Rebecca to marry me. But once I made *those* commitments, I realized I had made a mistake, because I *knew* that *strange world outside* the Amish community was going to claim me."

Exhausted . . . but relieved, he sighs and tenderly touches the side of Katherine's face. "Katherine, I deserved to be shunned . . . but if I had only known . . ." His words trail off as he thinks better of it.

Somewhat taken aback by what she has just heard, Katherine sits quietly for a moment, trying to absorb what her husband has shared with her. Not knowing what to say and realizing she has hit a raw nerve, perhaps even having gone too far, Katherine decides to change the mood. In a lighthearted manner she responds, "Well, I am a little concerned . . . !"

Royer, thinking about what she has just said, asks, "Concerned about *what?*"

Katherine chides back to him. "I'm concerned

about leaving those two kids alone at home . . . at their age."

Her ploy works as Royer thinks about that for a second, then cracks up laughing. "Jesus, Katherine, they're not even kissing cousins. Besides, Matthew wouldn't know what to do, even if it was right in front of his face."

Katherine gets up and smiling to her husband, says, "Oh, James Royer, you're terrible. But I guess that's why I love you and married you . . you're so damn sexy."

She's now behind his chair and starts to pull it out. "Come on, let's dance."

Royer playfully gets up and starts to lead her to the dance floor. Just then, all the lights go out leaving the room dark except for the candles on the tables. There is a surprised gasp from the members.

Over the garage in the guest room, Matthew, in his longjohns, is just crawling into bed when the lights on the nightstand go out. He's not that used to electricity so he just shrugs and continues to get into bed. Remembering, he gets out of bed and kneels beside it, silently saying his prayers.

When he is finished, he climbs back into bed and

puts his hands behind his head on the pillow and stares at the ceiling with the moonlight reflecting on it from the dormer windows.

Suddenly a strange light is flickering and Matthew turns and looks at the window. A light is moving and shining on it.

He gets up, goes over, and looks down. Alex, in a short nightshirt, is shining a flashlight up at him and the window.

With a slight appreciative smile, he opens the window and calls down to her. "Alex, you've got the custom all backwards . . ."

Alex, playfully rebuking him, teases back. "Matthew, the electricity has gone out and I thought you might need some candles." She holds them up. "I'll bring them up to you."

Before he can answer, Alex crosses over to the steps leading up to the guest room.

In the dark, Matthew is frantically looking around for his pants, but before he can locate them, Alex enters and her lovely young body is silhouetted by the moonlight. She closes the door behind her.

"I brought some matches . . . here, hold these."

Embarrassed, he gives up trying to step into the pants that he's finally located and takes the two candles Alex gives him, one in each hand. She strikes a match on the bedpost and lights the candles. "There, that's better."

Flickering, the candlelight does a seductive dance

on both their faces as they search each other's eyes with the voyage and thrill of discovery.

Pressing her body closer to him between his arms, Matthew looks helpless holding the two lit candles. He's never had feelings like this before and the urge to touch her overwhelms him. His frustrations mount not being able to take her in his arms.

She moves her lips closer to his and then teases him as she kisses his eyes, his cheek, his chin, and then back to his lips, where they finally meet in a devouring kiss. His emotions are now so strong he can hardly stand it any longer and his whole being feels as if it will melt.

Alex reaches out and takes the candles from Matthew's hands and places them on the nightstand. She slowly presses her body against his and onto the bed and whispers to him, "Show me how to bundle, Matthew."

His body is trembling now that his arms are free. He brings Alex to him gently. "I can't . . . we don't have a bundling board."

"We can use these . . ."

She reaches behind her for the pillows and places them between their two bodies. They start to kiss deeply and passionately.

Then Alex's hand reaches down and pulls one of the pillows out from between them. After a long moment, Matthew's hand reaches down and pulls out the other pillow.

In the candlelight, the pillows are thrown in the air and away from the bed as Alex and Matthew begin to make love.

In the dining room of the country club, additional candles have been brought in and the atmosphere is even more romantic than before.

The combo is playing the "Anniversary Waltz" while members are giving Katherine, nestled in Royer's arms, their moment on the dance floor.

Tenderly, Katherine says to her husband, "Happy anniversary, my darling."

Royer, with a loving smile, responds, "Happy anniversary to you, too, Katherine."

Trying again, she asks, "Are you happy you married me?"

Royer gives her a couple of extra twirls, trying to collect the dichotomy of his thoughts before answering. "God always gives us the right person in our lives at the right time."

He looks at her gently. "I love you, Katherine."

Katherine, willing to accept any straw, lays her head on his shoulder as the waltz comes to an end and the members applaud politely.

"Me, too . . ." Katherine kisses his cheek and snuggles even closer. Just then his telephone beeper goes off and the people around the dance floor react, as does Katherine. Extending her palms straight up, she says to them. "It's the story of my life."

They laugh as Royer takes Katherine back to their table and seats her.

"It must be a real emergency, because they know about tonight . . ." he sighs. He leaves quickly. "I'll be right back!"

Royer hurries out into the lobby where it's not hard to find a secluded place with the sparse candles lighting the area.

He takes out his cell phone and dials a number. "This is Royer . . ." He listens, and then urgently responds, "Okay . . . put the plan in action. I'll go directly there!"

He snaps the phone closed and hurries back into the dining room. At the entrance he stops and speaks to Robaire. Robaire looks toward Katherine and nods. Royer then quickly enters the dining room and crosses over to their table. By the expression on his face, Katherine knows what is coming.

Royer bends over, gives her a peck on the forehead, and quickly speaks. "I love you . . . I'm sorry about tonight. I'll make it up to you."

He is gone almost instantly.

Katherine's eyes follow her husband hurrying out of the room and she becomes aware that most members are also watching his departure. She takes a deep breath and turns the candle and its holder between her fingers. Sighing, she bends over and blows the candle out, then slowly gets up.

Just then, a pleasant looking couple stops by the table. It is Mary Lou, one of Katherine's socialite friends, and her husband, Paul. Trying to cheer her up, Mary Lou sincerely implores to her, "Katherine, come join our group . . . it's too early for you to go home."

Paul, nodding in agreement, adds, "Please, we'd love to have you." Then, taking her arm he reassures her, "We'll take you home."

"That would be nice. Thank you, Paul." Katherine moves off with them.

Chapter 21

Todd's truck is coming out of the gates of the warehouse. Heading down the darkly lit street, it approaches a corner and turns onto another street with light traffic.

Inside the pickup, with its dark tinted windows, Dino passes a bottle to Todd. They're both a little loaded.

"Thanks . . ." Todd takes a belt. "We'll drop my stuff off at my place first, then yours, and then we'll—*Holy shit!*"

Coming straight at them on the other side of the road is a Drug Enforcement Agency battering ram followed by an obvious flotilla of DEA agents and police cars.

Todd's truck is approaching a side ramp leading up the bridge over the river. Dino quickly looks out the rear window and sees other vehicles coming from the opposite direction, turning into the road leading to the warehouse.

"Christ! There's more of them coming from the other direction."

Turning back to Todd, he barks, "Fuck! Don't panic . . . just follow that car onto the bridge."

Todd picks up his speed considerably.

Dino shouts at him, "Slow up, asshole. Just drive normal!"

Todd's truck turns on the ramp and follows a car onto the bridge, while the DEA and police entourage continues on down the street to the road leading to the warehouse.

Looking ahead, Todd and Dino can't believe what they're seeing. In anger and frustration, Todd hits the top of the steering wheel with his fist. "Jesus, there's more!"

Moving at a fast pace and approaching them are three more vehicles—two squad cars followed by an unmarked car. As they pass, Todd and Dino see Royer driving his own car, still in his tux.

"Is that who I think it is!?" Todd cries out incredulously.

Squinting his eyes, Dino asks in amazement, "What the fuck's he wearing? Jeez, I hate that son of a bitch! My old man was right . . . when he had the chance, he should have blown him apart once and for all."

Dino takes a couple of large swigs from the bottle.

Looking behind them, they see the three cars speed down the ramp and turn toward the wharf.

On the street approaching the warehouse, silently and slowly moving with lights out, is the battering ram with the DEA and police cars following, two abreast. On a given signal, they pick up speed and turn on all their lights, heading for the heavily locked gates.

Inside the compound a frightened, armed guard hears a growing rumble which builds to a crescendo.

The battering ram crashes into the gates, sending them flying into the air.

Startled by the lights, the guard fires his Uzi at the huge rumbling machine. He fires another burst and runs toward the warehouse.

The DEA and police cars flood into the area behind the battering ram.

All hell breaks loose when a hood from the second floor window sprays them with his Uzi, sending the officers ducking for cover as they get out of their cars.

By now the guard has reached the door to the warehouse and turns and fires one last blast, but this time he's spun around in a hail of gunfire and goes down.

At the wharf are the parked speedboats with the men completing the loading. They grab weapons they have stashed when they hear the gunfire.

Reacting to all the noise and commotion, Salvatore comes running out of the warehouse along the dock.

"Get those boats out of here . . . *NOW!*"

In front of the warehouse, DEA men run up the ramp and start into the building.

Royer jumps out of his car amidst a hail of gunfire from the second floor window.

In the background, the DEA and police return the gunfire and, suddenly, a body crashes through the window and falls to the ground below.

On the bridge, inside Todd's pickup, Todd and Dino hear the various bursts of gunfire from the warehouse area below. In awe, Todd blurts out, "Fuck! I'm glad we're not down there!"

Dino points to an emergency parking area on the bridge. "Pull over! They don't know we're here."

Todd pulls the pickup over to the emergency parking area. Dino and Todd jump out and run to the railing.

With a bird's-eye view, they look down on the warehouse area below to a scene of pandemonium.

The battering ram and squad cars with their bubblegum lights cast an eerie, psychedelic effect over the entire area.

DEA men run into the warehouse, spraying bursts of gunfire everywhere.

Other policemen and DEA officers fan out and start down the long dock area toward the speedboats.

They see Royer being handed a bullhorn.

Below, Royer, in the midst of the chaos, is a strange sight in his tuxedo.

He shouts into the bullhorn. "Throw down your weapons . . . you have no chance! You're surrounded!"

At the loading area, Salvatore jumps from the dock into the middle speedboat as the first one takes off in a blast of power.

One of the hoods sprays an Uzi burst on the advancing officers running down the dock as they flatten out.

Salvatore grabs an Uzi and also sprays the dock area. "Like hell we're surrounded!"

Then, yelling at the hood driving the speedboat, "Get the fuck out of here!"

Salvatore's speedboat and the third one roar off. Almost simultaneously, bullets splatter the containers and pieces of the speedboat fly in the air.

Royer observes what's happening and moves to the closed end of the dock. He grabs his walkie-talkie and flicks the switch. "They're taking off!"

Admiral Sprague's voice is heard from the walkie-talkie. "We're here, Royer!"

The first speedboat races down the waterway between the docks toward the open end, headed for the freedom of the Delaware River.

The driver turns and looks back, then smiles when he sees the two other boats roar away from the dock.

Turning around, his face reflects sheer horror when he sees, directly in front of him, on the left side of the outlet, a Navy tug pushing a long flat barge perpendicular to the opening.

He tries to cut the power—but it's too late. At maximum speed, he crashes dead center of the empty barge, sending parts and a massive fireball high into the night sky and lighting up the whole area.

Up on the bridge, Dino and Todd's astonished faces light up from the explosion as the deafening boom reaches them.

Todd, in disbelief, "Jesus! Did you see . . . ?"

Dino, pointing excitedly. "My God . . . *LOOK!*"

Also being moved into place are two more Navy tugs pushing their long barges to the right side and middle of the outlet. A Navy frigate is directing the operation from behind the barges. They also see the second and third speedboats heading at full speed toward the river.

In the second speed boat, Salvatore hands the Uzi to the driver as he takes over the wheel and throttle.

The third speedboat on the right side is a little ahead of them and gaining more speed. The driver looks up; coming in on the right side and closing fast is the third long barge looming up in front of him.

He spins the wheel instantly to the left . . . the only thing he can do to avoid the fate of the first boat.

The third speedboat cuts in front of Salvatore's boat and almost slices it in two. Spinning around in a half circle, the third boat is now forced back down between the docks.

Salvatore's boat, from the wake of the third boat, becomes airborne and is thrown off course. To avoid hitting the barge, he has to make a loop around and is trapped going the wrong way.

The DEA and police open fire on one of the hoods who is blasting at them from the third speedboat. He is hit and knocked overboard, while the driver is also hit and slumps over the throttle.

The boat speeds out of control, full bore, to the closed end of the dock where Royer and some of the officers have been watching. Those on each side of Royer react and dive for cover.

True fear registers in Royer's eyes as the speedboat hits the lower landing of the dock and becomes airborne, heading right at him with the high-powered twin engine screws under the boat coming right at his head.

At that split second he dives for the ground and flattens himself enough not to be decapitated.

The speedboat, still climbing, flies over Royer. The other officers scramble out of the way as it crashes and explodes on top of the police cars.

On the bridge, Todd and Dino are in awe. Taking another swig from the bottle, Dino passes it to Todd. "Shit! That lucky asshole! Somebody will get him yet."

They hear a loud bullhorn from the bridge of the frigate as Admiral Sprague's voice bellows, "Turn back. Don't even try it!"

Todd reacts to his father's voice in disbelief. "Dad!?"

Dino points excitedly. "Look! They're closing the trap with all those Navy tugs and barges coming together!"

Below, Salvatore's speedboat heads straight at them.

On the bridge of the frigate, once again Admiral Sprague speaks into the bullhorn. "Cut your motors! You can't escape . . . You're blocked off!"

Salvatore feigns and somewhat cuts the motors to make his loop but now determined, he throws the speedboat into full throttle and defiantly yells, "Fuck you! The hell I am . . ."

Salvatore sees the trap closing, but there appears to still be room between the first and second barge for the speedboat to escape to the river.

His boat is moving so fast the screws are practically out of the water and flying between the end of the two barges.

He appears to have made it when, from the rig on each end of the barge, arms spring up raising a huge submarine net.

Sheer terror registers on Salvatore's face when he sees the huge steel submarine cables.

The front of the speedboat hits and pierces the net as Salvatore's body flies through the air and becomes deadly imbedded.

Like a giant sailfish caught in a net, the speedboat hopelessly fights for its life as the motors thrash and are finally silenced in the huge steel net.

Silence, too, up on the bridge for Dino and Todd, with the enormity of the moment sinking in. Looking over the railing, Todd finally speaks, "I wonder if he knows about me?"

Dino, alone with his thoughts, adds, "What difference does it make? We're fucked! My old man will never get out of prison now, and he'll blame it on me for the rest of his life."

Todd's eyes moisten. "Me, too . . ."

Dino looks down over the railing and in utter frustration yells, "That goddamned Royer!"

Turning to Todd, he commands, "Let's get out of here . . . I've got an idea to silence him forever!"

They head back to Todd's pickup. Dino downs the last swig of the bottle and tosses it back over his head into the river.

They get into the pickup and continue over the bridge.

Dino, his brain now in overdrive, says thoughtfully, "You used to go to high school with Royer's kid . . . right?"

"Yeah, I even took her out a couple of times," Todd remembers.

"You still have any shit left from the barns?" Dino asks.

"Yeah, more than half of it," Todd answers.

Dino, silent and still thinking, excitedly finally speaks out. "Bitchin! Let's get out of here!" Todd's pickup gains speed as it goes down the other side of the bridge.

Standing at the end of the dock, Royer watches the DEA agents bring a few hoods out of the warehouse. They are under guard, with their arms handcuffed behind their backs.

In the background, the Navy frigate pulls up behind the submarine net and the entwined boat.

With his tux ripped and dirty from his dive to the ground, Royer looks spent. He takes off his bow tie, pulls out his walkie-talkie, and looks at the frigate. "Thanks, Admiral, for your cooperation and one hell of a job."

On the bridge, Admiral Sprague, too, is exhausted and extremely worried. Speaking into his walkie-talkie he asks, "Royer . . . is he alive?"

Concerned, Royer responds to the commander. "Admiral, I'm sorry you had to find out about Todd this way . . . but I don't think your son or the Bertolli kid were here."

For a second, the Admiral is relieved, then he

pleads, "Royer . . . try to bring him in alive." His voice chokes. "He's all I have left."

Royer, emotionally drained, answers, "I'll do my best, Admiral."

Chapter 22

Todd's pickup slows at the entrance gates to the Royer home. The headlights flick off and silently the wide body creeps up the driveway.

Inside the truck, Dino is putting a clip in a gun and looking at the house. Then quietly to Todd, "That's weird . . . there're no lights on."

"Yeah, I noticed that...there're no lights on in the whole area."

Dino points to some trees near the end of the house. "Pull in there."

Todd pulls off the driveway and parks under the trees. He shuts off the motor.

The candles have burned lower on the nightstand in Matthew's guest room over the garage.

Alex is cuddled in Matthew's arms, and the after-glow is evident in both of them as she plays with his long hair with one finger.

She sighs. "I'd better get back before the folks get home."

Neither one wants to move. Matthew gently touches her face. "Yah, you're right."

Alex raises up on one elbow. "Matthew . . . ?"

Matthew, not wanting to break the mood. "Ummm . . ."

She playfully kisses the end of his nose. "I have a confession to make . . . it's the first time I've ever *bei-schlofed* too."

Matthew raises up on one elbow and looks at Alex. "Really?"

"Really. . ." She playfully pulls his elbow out from under him and starts to get out of bed.

Dino and Todd silently get out of the truck. Todd reaches back and takes some rope and a roll of tape off the seat, then reaches below and grabs a crowbar. He gently closes the door, trying to not make any sound.

They move off cautiously toward the back of the house.

Alex is now sitting on the edge of the bed, putting on her nightshirt. Matthew, on the other side, is slipping back into his longjohns.

Going over toward the door, Alex stops for a moment before opening it to leave.

"Wait . . . I'll walk you," Matthew pleads.

He stands and slips into his pants.

"You don't have to do that." Alex is touched.

"No, I want to."

Matthew presents quite a picture in bare feet, longjohn top, and Amish black baggy pants.

Helplessly enamored, he crosses to the door and opens it for Alex.

Looking at her sensuous body in the moonlight, he softly gasps, "You're beautiful . . ."

Alex, radiant and smiling, playfully responds, "And you, Matthew, are adorable."

They kiss and start down the stairs.

On the far side of the pool house and terrace, Dino with his gun, and Todd with a crowbar, ropes, and tape, cautiously move through the trees and bushes toward the main house and terrace.

They stop in their tracks when they hear muffled voices. Creeping closer alongside the pool house, they see two forms come down the steps from the guest house above the garage.

Alex and Matthew cross by the pool and reach the French doors leading into the main house. Alex opens them and turns back to Matthew.

Dino and Todd are watching from behind a hedge.

Matthew is struggling for words, then finally. "Alex . . . ah . . ."

Just then the lights go back on.

Startled, Dino blurts out, "What the *fuck!?*"

Matthew and Alex are doubly surprised and frightened when they turn and see Dino stepping onto the terrace with a gun pointed at them, followed by Todd carrying a menacing crowbar.

Dino, desperate, barks out, "Don't move!"

Dino and Todd move in.

Dino gruffly snaps at Alex, "Where's your mother?"

Alex looks at Todd and recognizes him. "Todd, what are you . . . ?"

Dino impatiently cuts her off. "Shut up . . . and just answer!"

"She's not here . . ." Alex answers, frightened and her voice breaking.

Dino, disappointed. "That's too bad."

He walks over to Matthew, poking his gun into his chest. "He'll do!"

Now, recognizing Matthew, he snidely adds, "Well, if it isn't our very own strip joint horny Romeo!"

He surveys Matthew and laughs. "I must say, you do get around for an Amishman."

Todd whirls around and is also surprised at seeing Matthew's face. "How the hell did you get out of jail, you murdering bastard?"

Dino suddenly brightens with an idea. "Better yet! We'll fix them right in their fucking Amish own back-yard . . . the same place they got my old man."

Dino gives off a maniacal laugh, "Poetic justice!" He turns to Todd and commands, "Tape up their mouths and wrists!"

Dino holds his gun on the terrified kids as Todd quickly puts tape over their mouths. He then tapes their hands behind their backs.

Seeing they're secured, Dino puts his gun away, takes something out of his jacket and heads into the house.

"Watch them!" he orders.

Todd picks up the crowbar and taps it menacingly on his palm. Alex and Matthew, mouths taped, can only stare in wide-eyed disbelief at what is happening to them.

Walking into the entry hall, Dino quickly goes to the telephone stand and picks up a pen. Hurriedly, he scribbles something on a paper he's taken out of his jacket. He also copies down the telephone number from the phone.

Dino gets up and looks around, trying to decide where to put the paper. He spots the entry stairs and lays the paper on the first step. Quickly he leaves and comes out onto the terrace. "Come on . . . move it!"

He starts shoving Alex and Matthew toward the pool house. "We're out of here!"

Dino grabs Alex by the arm and Todd yanks Matthew by the hair, while quickly leading them to the pickup.

At the truck, they shove Alex and Matthew into the back seat and then climb in. Todd rapidly backs onto the driveway and burns rubber as they tear out of there.

Paul, driving his Rolls Royce, comes down the road toward the Royer home. He sees a wide-bodied pick-up truck passing in the opposite direction driving at a reckless speed. He mutters under his breath to himself, "Damn kids with those things . . . think they own the road!"

Katherine is in the back seat with Mary Lou. They are both turned towards each other and deep into their conversation.

"I don't know if I could do it." Mary Lou is shaking her head.

Katherine fatalistically sighs, "I hate it, but what can I tell you . . . I love the guy."

After a long pause, she finishes. "I die a little each time he leaves . . . not knowing."

Paul turns into the driveway. Seeing all the lights on, he remarks, "Looks like Alex is having a party."

Katherine, concerned, replies, "Shouldn't be, at this hour . . ."

Paul pulls up to the steps and starts to get out. Katherine puts a hand on his shoulder as she gets out from the back seat. "Don't bother, Paul, and thanks for the ride and evening. Good night, Mary Lou."

Katherine hurries up the stairs as Mary Lou calls, "I'll check with you tomorrow."

Katherine waves and gets her keys out. She enters the house and Paul drives away.

Upon entering, she puts her keys away and notices the doors open leading to the patio. She calls up the stairs. "Alex . . . Alex, are you there?"

She crosses, looks out the back, and sees Matthew's guest room lights on. Katherine shrugs, then closes the doors and starts up the steps. She notices a piece of paper on the first step and stops to pick it up. She hears a car pull up, turns, and looks out.

Getting out of his car and carrying his tux jacket, Royer hurries up the steps.

He is surprised when the front door opens for him

and Katherine frowns. "You look awful . . . are you all right?"

Royer gives her a kiss on the cheek and throws his jacket on a chair. He heads for the service bar in the living room. "What a night . . . I need a drink!"

Katherine follows him in. "What an anniversary . . ."

He fixes his drink. "Sorry about that. We'll celebrate tomorrow night. Want one?"

"No thanks." She shakes her head.

He takes a huge gulp of his drink and then looks around. "What are all the lights on for?"

"I don't know. Paul and Mary Lou just dropped me off from the club."

He notices the paper in her hand, and takes another good chug of his drink. "What's that?"

Katherine looks down, surprised. She had forgotten she had it in her hand. She looks over at Royer and answers. "It was on the steps . . ."

She opens the folded paper and begins reading aloud:

> "ROYER - IF YOU EVER WANT TO
> SEE YOUR DAUGHTER AND AMISH
> KID ALIVE AGAIN YOU'D . . ."

Katherine's face turns ashen. "Oh, no! Oh, God no!"

Royer hurries to her and snaps the paper out of her hands. He takes one look and then runs to the stairs and bounds up. "*ALEX! ALEX*! Are you there?"

Katherine, in a panicked state of shock, runs to the patio doors and throws them open, screaming up at the guest room, *"MATTHEW! MATTHEW! ALEX! Answer us . . . PLEASE . . . !"*

She starts to sob hysterically as Royer races back down the stairs and takes her in his arms. He brings her back into the house.

Chapter 23

The truck weaves slightly as it speeds down the road through the Amish countryside.

Dino passes a half-consumed new bottle of booze to Todd while he drives. "Seeing that bastard Royer likes to blow people up so much . . . he'll get his in 'Kingdom Come!'"

Todd then asks quizzically, "Where'd you learn so much about explosives?"

In the back seat, Alex and Matthew listen wide-eyed and apprehensively to the frightening dialogue coming from their captors. Alex is still in her nightshirt and Matthew is still in his longjohns and pants. With their mouths taped, they are a pathetic sight.

Dino answers Todd's question in a somewhat bragging tone. "In the army, before I got booted out."

Through the windshield, Dino notices a road to the

side that is under construction and blocked off with all kinds of caution signs. "Pull over! We're gonna need some of those!" he orders Todd.

Todd slams on the brakes. The truck skids to a crazy stop, and then he backs up.

Dino jumps out. He runs to a couple of orange and white sawhorses that have a "Road Closed" sign attached and tosses them in the back of the pickup. Then he scoops up and piles on top of one another several orange cones that are used to block off lanes and throws them in.

Spotting two "Detour" signs with arrows, he picks them up and drops them in the back of the truck, adding to the stash he just collected.

Climbing back into the truck, he snaps at Todd, "Let's get moving!"

Todd obediently responds by downing the throttle, sending rocks and pebbles flying as the pickup roars down the pike.

In the kitchen-family room of the Royer home, the phone sits on an island counter in the center of the kitchen.

Pacing, Katherine nervously tries to drink some coffee while holding the saucer in the other hand.

Royer is on the edge of a breakfast nook chair staring at the phone, while subconsciously pounding the paper in his hand.

"Don't be a hero and get them killed!" Katherine pleads.

Obviously agitated, Royer responds to her statement. "We *can't* keep waiting! I've got to let headquarters know . . . we have procedures for . . ."

Katherine, her voice now rising, frantically cuts him off. "But I've heard you tell me on kidnapping cases like this, sometimes things go wrong . . . mistakes are made!"

Frustrated, Royer gets up and paces like a trapped animal.

"It's sure as *hell different* when it's your own kids!" He realizes he made a slip of the tongue, and looks at Katherine. In her frantic state, she's not aware of his words.

He *slams* his fist down on the counter next to the phone. *"RING, YOU BASTARDS!"*

On the familiar country road with an Amish farm in the background, Todd's pickup speeds toward the wooden bridge and trees near the entrance road to the Ammann farm.

In the back seat of the pickup, Matthew nudges Alex with his body, and with panicked eyes, nods toward the left as they enter the bridge. Coming out the other side, he nods again to his lane.

Alex frowns, not understanding what Matthew is trying to tell her.

The truck continues on over a slight rise.

Through the windshield, Todd and Dino see that they are fast approaching a "T" in the road.

Dino shouts, "Stop . . . right here!"

Todd slams on the brakes and skids to a stop. Dino jumps out and takes one of the "Road Closed" sawhorses and sets it up in the middle of the road. He runs back and grabs four of the orange cones and one "Detour" sign with an arrow.

Dino blocks the rest of the road with the cones and then stands the "Detour" sign pointing in the opposite direction.

Hurriedly, he runs and jumps back in the pickup. "Back up and head back!"

Todd whips the truck around and speeds back over the rise. He slows down and parks under the tree near the covered bridge and shuts out the lights. They both jump out and start unloading supplies, carrying them to the covered bridge.

Matthew and Alex, bound, gagged, and locked in the back seat, can only watch as Dino starts to climb under the bridge with his load. Todd, arms full, enters the bridge with his bundle.

Now, realizing what they intend to do, Matthew panics, and with a guttural sound, motions to Alex at the open window on the driver's side. He struggles to climb over the cab seat, but with his arms tied behind him and the tight quarters, it's almost impossible. Alex tries to help him by pushing her body against his.

Meanwhile under the bridge, Dino is deftly attaching small bundles with tape while moving among the wooden braces.

Todd, inside the bridge, has climbed up in the wooden trusses. He, too, is attaching his packages to the beams.

Matthew, now partially stuck between the top of the seat and the cab roof, has his head down on the driver's side. Alex tries to push his legs up and over to unwedge him.

Dino has finished and climbs up from under the bridge.

Inside, Todd completes his job and swings down to the bridge planking and joins Dino. "Let's get to the phone and start the *'Big Show!'*"

They turn and head toward the pickup.

Through the windshield, a terrified Alex sees Dino and Todd heading back. She gives Matthew a muffled warning and a frantic push. His head and shoulders jolt forward and jam into the steering wheel and horn.

The loud horn blares, startling Dino and Todd. They begin running to the pickup.

Matthew struggles to free himself, but to no avail.

The horn continues to wail as Dino and Todd reach the car and throw open the door on the driver's side.

Dino lets out a sadistic laugh when he sees Matthew's predicament. "Had to have a front row seat, huh?"

He grabs Matthew's long hair with one hand and with the other hand on his shoulder shoves him back into Alex in the back seat, hissing, "Don't worry, you'll both be part of the show soon enough!"

Dino and Todd jump into the front seat and start the motor. Burning rubber, they approach the bridge and drive through, heading back down the road.

Chapter 24

In the kitchen-family room, with their positions reversed, Royer is nervously pacing with a coffee mug in his hand, and Katherine is seated with her arms on the counter with her body rocking.

Staring at the phone, she can no longer hold back and almost hysterically screams. "I can't stand anymore of this! We've got to do something!"

With a sigh of resignation, he replies, "They could be anywhere by now . . ."

He pulls up a chair next to Katherine and puts his arm around her to help soothe and quiet her. "Right now, there's nothing we can do . . ."

Then, with almost a plea and quietly to himself, he adds, "I hope to God I didn't make a mistake and wait too long."

In the headlights of the pickup and coming toward them is an open buggy with a big, lone Amish kid driving. It is Amos.

Dino gets a bright idea and excitedly says to Todd, "Perfect! A buggy! Just what we need . . . stop it and cut him off!"

Todd slows and pulls right up in front of the frightened horse, blinding him and forcing Amos to stop.

Dino jumps out and approaches the buggy. "Sorry, Pal . . . I need your horse and buggy for awhile."

Suddenly he recognizes Amos who had fallen on him and had him spread-eagled on the sidewalk in front of the strip joint. Sarcastically, he confronts Amos. "Well, if it isn't my ole' Amish asshole buddy!"

Amos sits silently in his buggy, holding his whip.

Then Dino, with mock sweetness, adds, "You'll loan me your buggy . . . right!?"

Amos responds defiantly. "Nah, not *my* horse and buggy."

Dino moves threateningly closer to the buggy. Amos stands up, twisting the whip in his hands.

Dino daringly says, "Go ahead . . ."

Inside the pickup Todd watches, amused, while Matthew in the back seat recognizes Amos and is fearfully concerned knowing how stubborn the Pennsylvania Dutch can be.

The headlights of the truck light up the buggy and Dino moves closer. " . . . Use it . . . I dare you . . . !" Dino taunts.

Amos, true to his Amish nonviolent beliefs and his nature, drops the whip to the ground in front of Dino.

"Fucking coward!" Dino reaches in his jacket and in a flash, pulls out his gun and fires twice, blasting Amos right out of the buggy into the ditch.

A startled Todd yells, *"JESUS!"* His hand jerks up covering his mouth in stunned surprise.

Matthew, in shocked disbelief at seeing what has happened to his buddy, is on the verge of throwing up but can't with the tape over his mouth. He can only moan and wretch with pain like a wounded animal.

Alex, terrified at what she just witnessed sobs uncontrollably then suddenly stops, her heart paralyzed in fear. Through the windshield she sees Dino calmly walking back to the pickup with the gun in his hand. He goes to Matthew's side of the pickup and opens the door.

Matthew and Alex now have new panic in their eyes.

Dino casually reaches in and unties the rope around Matthew's ankles then reaches up and tears the tape off his wrists that are tied behind his back.

"Come on . . . get out!" he commands.

Matthew stumbles out of the truck and Dino motions him to the buggy with the gun.

"Always wanted to ride in one of these things," Dino laughs in a maniacal tone.

Alex watches through the windshield in petrified fear for Matthew.

Todd, now with a twinge that things have gone too far, hears Dino bellow at Matthew, "Get in and drive it!"

He turns and gestures to Todd. "Follow us . . . !"

Dino and Matthew climb into the buggy. Matthew takes the reins and starts to turn the horse around. He wants to look in the ditch to see if Amos is still alive, but is too afraid to and starts down the road.

Todd, doing as he is told, follows in the pickup, lighting up the horse and buggy from behind.

Laughing, Dino turns around and waves to Todd. "Just like a buggy ride at Disneyland!"

Inside Rebecca and Hans' bedroom, Rebecca, unable to sleep, is concerned about Matthew and is wide awake. She looks toward the open window while Hans tosses.

He, too, can't sleep. He turns toward her and notices she's awake. "Rebecca, it's late . . . you've got to get some rest."

"Hans, did you hear that noise a minute ago? It sounded like two gun shots," Rebecca asks, worried.

Hans yawns and rolls over. "It was probably backfire from an old Mennonite car . . . Rebecca, go to sleep."

Chapter 25

Outside Zimmerman's Grocery Store in Intercourse, the town is dark and completely deserted at that hour.

The commandeered horse and buggy are tied to a hitching rail, and Todd's pickup is parked out of range of the one light source on the porch.

Inside the pickup, Matthew, mouth and wrists now once again taped, can only watch in fear.

Dino unties Alex's ankles, then reaches up and pulls the tape off her mouth but leaves her arms taped behind her.

Dino roughly pulls her out and with a threatening voice in her ear says, "One fucking scream, one wrong word, and you're *BOTH DEAD! Got it?*"

Alex nods, wide-eyed and frightened, as Dino leads her up to the phone booth on the porch while keeping her tightly next to him. He reaches in his pocket and pulls out a piece of paper. He dials a number and waits, then drops in some coins.

In the Royer living room, Katherine sits on the couch and Royer is in an armchair nearby with his head back and one leg over the arm. A long cord reaches the phone on the coffee table between them. *IT RINGS!*

Katherine and Royer jump from the shock. He grabs it with an urgent, *"HELLO!"*

He hears Dino gruffly order, "Royer . . . now *listen* and *listen good* if you want to see them alive. Go to the phone booth at Zimmerman's in Intercourse and your next instructions will be taped under the shelf of the phone!"

Royer anxiously asks, "Zimmerman's at Intercourse . . . *WAIT!* What do you *want?*"

"You'll find out soon enough!" Dino snaps back.

Royer, now trying to calm down, continues, "How do I know they're alive?"

Dino shoves the phone up to Alex's mouth. She desperately pleads into the phone. "Be careful, Jim . . . they're *crazy!* They just *KILLED . . .*"

Dino yanks the phone away. "Hear that, Royer? You'd better fucking follow all the instructions to the letter and not one sight of anyone but you, or they're *DEAD MEAT!*"

"WAIT!" he cries desperately. It's too late. Royer slowly puts the phone down and turns to Katherine. Frantically, she looks at him, her eyes pleading.

At the phone booth by Zimmerman's, Dino takes a piece of paper out of his pocket and scribbles some additional instructions on it and tapes it under the ledge.

He then yanks Alex toward the pickup and shoves her back in.

Matthew looks on helplessly as Dino quickly retapes her mouth.

Todd pulls away and turns onto the road leading to the covered bridge.

"Stop!" Dino yells.

Todd complies and Dino jumps out and goes to the flatbed and gathers up the remaining construction signs.

Matthew and Alex look out the back window and see Dino set up the "Road Closed" cones and "Detour" sign and arrow. He then jumps back in the truck and Todd roars off.

Matthew and Alex in the backseat, can only communicate helpless concern for one another through their eyes. When the pickup approaches the area where Amos was blown off his buggy, they look to see if his body is in the ditch, but it's too dark. Once again their fear takes over.

As the pickup nears the covered bridge, Dino instructs Todd, "Slow down and stop just inside the entrance."

Doing as he's told, Todd stops the pickup.

Dino climbs up into the bed of the truck, takes a spool of fine wire and reaches up to a wooden beam where Todd has taped a package. Dino untapes it and wraps the wire around the package, then secures the wire with the tape. When he is finished, Dino carefully lifts the package over the beam and lets it dangle just below the beam by the wire. He cautiously climbs out of the bed of the pickup with the roll of wire.

Barking another order, he shouts to Todd, "Pull ahead to the other end!"

Todd pulls away to the other end as instructed. Dino goes over to the open railing post on his left side and, about two feet off the ground, puts the roll of wire behind it, then crosses perpendicular to the railing post on the opposite side and slips the wire roll behind it. He then runs the length of the bridge, letting out the wire. When he gets to the end of the bridge, he climbs up into the bed of the pickup with the roll of wire.

In the back window, Matthew and Alex strain to see as Dino repeats attaching the wire to a package, letting it dangle over the beam. After he finishes, he cuts the wire from the roll and jumps back into the truck.

Pointing ahead to the rise in the road, he shouts, "We'd better get to our front row seats to see the show!"

Todd starts the pickup and moves out laughing, "Starring *JAMES ROYER!*"

Dino pulls the bottle out from under the seat and takes a swig. Then, like an announcer, with his arm he gestures, "The world's biggest asshole in his *LAST PERFORMANCE!*"

The truck pulls off toward some trees in a field at the top of the hill. It circles and pulls in under the branches facing the covered bridge and road.

Todd shuts off the motor and Dino passes him the bottle. He puts his head back on the seat and smugly adds, "Now all we have to do is wait . . ."

Todd, downing a swig, finishes for him, " . . . until the *CURTAIN GOES UP!*"

With the Dutch masters' single light source from the crescent moon, the Currier and Ives setting, the covered bridge with its sides hinged up for summer, the moon glistening on the sleepy river below and the road like a ribbon lacing the lush hills of the Amish countryside, it's beautiful . . . except for the taped faces and terrified expressions of Matthew and Alex, which belie the beauty and silence of the moment.

Royer's car screeches to a halt at the steps leading to the porch of Zimmerman's. He jumps out leaving the motor running and hurries to the phone booth. Reaching under the shelf, he pulls out a folded piece of paper, takes the tape off, and reads the contents.

Royer, eyes flashing, can't hold back his rage. "They *damn well wouldn't!*"

He reads some more, then slowly turns around and scans the area past his car. He sees the horse and buggy tied to the hitching rail.

He warily looks around, folds the paper, and puts it in his pocket. Walking to his car, he reaches in and shuts the motor off, checks his handgun, and fills his pockets with bullets from a box. He then reaches across and grabs the shotgun on the seat and another box of shells and closes the door.

Royer slowly walks to the horse and buggy and lays the shotgun and box of shells on the seat. Then cautiously, he goes to the rail and unties the reins. The horse shies. In a loud reassuring whisper, he tries to calm him. "Whoa, boy!"

With all the skills of an ex-Amishman, he swings up into the buggy, turns the horse around, and slaps the reins. The animal responds and takes off down the street.

At the intersection and road leading to the bridge, Royer slows the horse and looks at the "Road Closed" signs. He brings the buggy to a stop under the lone overhead light, pulls out the folded paper, and double checks.

Royer reads the paper to himself. "Go past 'Road Closed' signs to 'Covered Bridge' . . . tree on other side has next instructions."

He gets out of the buggy and moves aside a couple of orange cones. He gets back in the buggy and guides the horse through. Then Royer, horse, and buggy take off at a trot down the road toward the bridge.

Chapter 26

On the rise of the hill above the covered bridge, Todd and Dino have their heads back resting while watching the road ahead.

Matthew and Alex, realizing the horror of what Dino and Todd have planned for Royer, in desperation have their bodies leaning forward slightly and turned away from each other. With their fingers they try to pull the tape off each other's wrists, without causing any movement or suspicion from Dino and Todd, whose heads are practically right there.

Todd finishes another swig from the bottle. With a worried slur he blurts out, "He should be here by now!"

"Don't worry . . . he's probably just putting on his makeup." Dino laughs at his own stupid joke.

Suddenly Matthew's eyes widen and he nudges

Alex. She sees it too. In the distance on the road is a moving object, too small to make out.

Dino turns his head to the side and glances back. "How's our two love birds do . . ."

He notices their reaction and whips his head around. Sitting straight up, Dino looks and sees the same object coming toward them. "Well now . . that's more like it. There's our *STAR!*"

Todd jolts up, excited.

Through the windshield, they all see Royer and the horse and buggy on the road in the distance, getting closer.

Todd is hardly able to contain himself.

"The *curtain* is about to *go up!*"

Dino flips out of his side of the pickup and starts to run down the field toward the bridge and trees. He calls back in wild anticipation, "That ain't all that's *GOING UP!*"

Caught up in the moment, Todd gets out and excitedly follows Dino, shouting, "Last call . . . Everyone take their seats!"

Practically standing up in the buggy, Royer slaps the reins urging the horse on. The horse responds with nostrils flaring as his head moves to the cadence of a fast trot.

Inside the pickup, Matthew, only able to make guttural sounds, panics as he pushes his body against Alex to move her over and give him room. She does as Matthew lays his head in her lap and stretches out across the seat. Alex at first doesn't understand what he is trying to do until she sees his bare toes trying to get hold of the door latch. He tries desperately to get leverage and a toehold but he can't quite do it in the position they're in, and his toes slip off.

Frantically, Matthew turns over and puts his face down in Alex's lap and stretches his legs backward to the latch. This time Matthew has the right position as his toes go up underneath the latch. He pulls his legs up and the latch and door pop open.

Matthew and Alex, with their arms still taped behind them, slide out of the truck to the ground. In doing so they panic and the door swings shut, causing an unwanted slam.

From the tree and bridge, Dino and Todd react to the noise. Looking up, they see Alex and Matthew trying to get their footing and escape.

Matthew and Alex start to run with their arms tied behind them.

Dino and Todd take off after them, and it isn't long before Todd tackles Alex and Dino catches Matthew, throwing him to the ground.

They are all panting from running.

Dino grinds his foot into Matthew's chest angrily. "You wouldn't want to miss the *BIG SHOW !?*" He yanks Matthew to his feet, and continues on, "...now, would you, Amish shithead?"

Todd has gotten Alex up off the ground and starts shoving her toward the pickup. Dino yells to him with a sadistic laugh, "Grab that rope . . . I've got a better idea!"

He starts to shove Matthew toward the bridge. "And bring *her* down. We're going to make them part of the show!"

Deep in thought, Royer stares at the road ahead and slaps the reins. The loud sound of the horse's hooves and the wheels' metal rims grinding on the pavement are accented with the horse's heavy breathing.

In the far distance, Royer looks ahead and can make out the outline of the covered bridge.

Under the bridge, Matthew and Alex are being tied to the underpinning by Todd, with Dino supervising.

Matthew struggles, trying to protest. He mutters guttural sounds through the tape.

"Oh, you want something!?" snarls Dino.

He takes out his gun and hits Matthew across the face with it. "Here!"

Todd, beginning to have second thoughts, reluctantly confronts Dino. "Dino, this is getting out of hand!"

Dino, now furious, shouts back, "Shut the *fuck* up, and *do what you're told!*"

Todd puts the last hitch around Alex. Their eyes meet . . . hers with a plea. Todd slips a pocketknife into Alex's palm as Dino calls angrily, "Hurry up!"

Dino starts to climb up the bank with his back to Alex and Matthew. With a snide laugh, he adds, "We don't want to go up with the curtain!"

Todd gives Matthew a sympathetic look as he passes and quickly tries to loosen the end of the rope that's around Matthew.

Dino turns and looks back. Impatiently, he snaps to Todd, "Come on! What the hell are you doing?"

Todd, now truly frightened, answers quickly. "Just checking to make sure it's tight."

Todd quickly scrambles up the bank and joins Dino as they take cover behind the tree.

Todd starts to tremble, then shakes when he sees Royer's approaching buggy getting closer. The enormity of what's about to take place sinks in.

Dino, furious, yells at Todd, "What's the *matter with you*!? You going *soft* on me?"

Todd, now really scared and panicked, looks and edges toward the dirt road behind him. He tries to speak, stammering nervously. "Dino, this is insane. This is . . ."

Dino is now out of control and whips out his gun. "You bastard! Are you calling me *crazy!?*"

He starts waving the gun wildly at Todd. "I'll show you who's *CRAZY!*"

Cracking, Todd starts frantically running up the lane and hill toward the Ammann farm.

Dino slowly raises the gun with an insane smile.

Todd is nearing the crest of the hill, running for all he is worth when Dino fires and hits Todd in the back. He staggers, falling face down in the dirt.

The crack of the whip hits the horse's back as Royer urges him on.

"Haa! Haa!" The horse responds to Royer's commands and picks up the pace.

Suddenly, Royer reacts when he looks ahead and sees the tree on the other side of the covered bridge, which is now looming in front of him.

Under the bridge, Matthew and Alex hear the approaching buggy.

Matthew frantically cuts through the last remaining rope with the knife that Alex has managed to slip into his hands. They struggle to free themselves while at the same time trying to tear the tape from their mouths to try to warn Royer. They finally break free and start to run from under the bridge.

Dino reacts in glee to the sound of Royer's approaching buggy. He turns and quickly moves back behind the tree and sees Royer, at a fast clip, closing in on the bridge.

Dino, like a cat watching a mouse, low and sadistically, mutters to himself, "Come on . . . come on baby. Just a little bit further."

Royer's buggy is now blocked from view by the end of the bridge. He again starts to slap the reins. Suddenly he gets an intuitive feeling as he looks up and tries to pull in on the reins with one hand and grabs his gun with the other. "Covered bridge . . . *SHIT!*"

The covered bridge looms over him just as he is starting to enter. The horse senses the wire and starts to shy, but it's too late as they move through the bridge snapping the wire and dropping the bundle behind them.

Royer dives off the buggy over the railing just as a tremendous explosion and fireball catches up to him in midair.

Dino watches the explosion, which is instantly followed by another massive booming blast and fireball at his end of the bridge.

Wounded and bleeding, Todd struggles to his feet. He reacts to the blast and turns to see the rest of the bridge explode into the air as the various booming charges go off, illuminating the night sky like Roman candles. Todd, in utter despair, mutters, "Oh, God, no . . ."

Rebecca and Hans wake up to the huge explosions and the glow from the fireball lights up their bedroom. They run to the window. Rebecca, in anguish, puts her hand to her face and exclaims, "It must be a plane crash!"

Hans moves away from the window with the sky still aglow.

"It's somewhere near the bridge! They'll need help. I'll get the wagon."

He throws on his pants and Rebecca quickly slips on her dress.

Dino, at the bridge, is in awe of his handiwork and

steps out from behind the tree. He moves toward the smoking ruins at the end of the bridge to survey the scene.

Momentarily stunned with burning debris all around him, Royer drags himself out of the water on the far side and starts to climb up the bank.

Below the bridge, near an underpinning and cross beam, flames are nearing an unexploded package. Dino's face appears as he looks out over the remains of the bridge and in excited glee shouts, "Now I'll tell you, Royer, what I want . . . *I WANTED YOUR DEAD ASS!*" Then, raising his fist, "This is for you, *Dad . . .*"

Royer with his vision finally clearing, looks over to the side of him and sees what's happening, and yells to Dino, "*GET BACK!*"

Startled, Dino reacts. "What the . . ."

Shocked, he turns and sees Royer. Instantly he pulls out his gun and fires at Royer.

Royer instinctively ducks, takes aim, and shoots. Dino, mortally wounded, staggers forward just as the unexploded package goes off, blowing him into the air.

Chapter 27

At the Ammann farm, Hans comes out of the barn with the wagon. Rebecca runs across from the house and turns to the children, who have come out on the porch.

"Elizabeth, look after Mary and Jacob. Ring the bell!"

Rebecca jumps up next to Hans, and they take off at a gallop around the side of the barn as the children race to the bell rope and start ringing it frantically.

In the lane in front of the house, a wounded and bleeding Todd staggers, trying to reach the farm for help. He hears the sound of the approaching wagon and horse's hooves, but can't move fast enough to get out of the way.

Hans whips the horse as it gallops around the corner of the barn. Much to his shock, he sees Todd and pulls back on the reins as hard as he can. Todd looks up to see the horse wide-eyed and looming above him. Pawing the air, Hans yanks the horse to a stop, inches from Todd's face.

Hans and Rebecca jump down and rush to Todd. As they start to assist him, Hans asks urgently, "Are there any others?"

Todd struggles to answer, but loses consciousness. Hans and Rebecca carefully lift him in their arms and carry him into the house.

Inside a police helicopter, Darren sits next to the pilot. In the back are a couple of other officers. They all look down anxiously as Darren spots something.

"Over there!"

Through the Plexiglas windshield, they see the smoldering fires and smoke from the remains of the bridge on the outskirts of Intercourse. The helicopter turns and nears.

Shocked and surprised at the enormity of what he sees, Darren reacts instantly. "My God! Quick, land over there in that clearing, as near to the bridge as you can get."

As they come down to land, they see a body spread-eagled on top of the road near the end of the bridge with someone leaning over it.

Darren mutters to himself, "I hope we're not too late!"

Royer is staring down at Dino's eyes, still open in a state of disbelief. His hand reaches over and shuts Dino's eyes.

Royer suddenly becomes aware of the sound of the police helicopter landing nearby and stands up, reacting to what is going on around him.

Darren and the officers jump down from the chopper and run over to the grisly scene. Recognizing Royer, and relieved to see he is still alive, Darren quickly asks him, "Jim, are you all right?"

Still somewhat in a state of shock, Royer, surprised at seeing Darren, responds, "Darren . . . how did you get here?"

Darren assists Royer to his feet. "Not long after you left, Katherine called us."

Suddenly, Royer remembers. *"ALEX! MATTHEW! My God! I hope they weren't in the bridge!"*

Panicked, he starts to run toward the bridge, but spots the truck under the trees.

"There's a pickup parked . . . just maybe . . ."

Then, desperately, he adds, "I'll check it out!"

Darren and the officers start to fan out on the banks and river, searching among the smoldering debris.

The helicopter, its red, blue, and white lights circling on top, throws an eerie glow over the deathly scene as Amish people arrive from all directions on foot, wagons, and buggies. Approaching in the distance is the old fire engine and two police cars.

Inside Rebecca and Hans' living room, Todd has been placed on the plain couch. The kerosene lanterns on the mantle sparsely light the room as Rebecca, with a basin of water, cleans and bathes Todd's wounds. Todd, in his delirium, mumbles, "Dad . . . please Dad, just listen to me. Please . . . !"

He drifts off and loses consciousness.

Hans is at the end of the sofa watching.

Elizabeth enters, out of breath and carrying a lantern. "Brother Hockstetler said he would be right here, Father."

"Good girl . . . thank you, Elizabeth," Hans replies.

Holding the lantern, she comes up on the other side of Hans, Mary and Jacob.

Running up to the parked truck on the ridge, Royer looks in. Seeing no one he hurriedly starts to return to the bridge but his eye catches several buggies pulling up to the Ammann farm. He quickly jumps into the pickup, starts it, and speeds down across the field toward the farmhouse.

In the Ammann living room, the flickering light from the lantern illuminates all their Amish faces.

Hans softly speaks. "All we can do now is pray."

They all kneel and look respectfully at Todd.

Rebecca puts down her basin and also kneels.

Hans' voice and hand gestures give the words new meaning.

>"Our Father, who art in heaven,
>· Hallowed be thy name.
>Thy kingdom come,
>Thy will be . . ."

Todd stirs, comes to, and through his blurred vision sees their caring faces and hears,

>" . . . done,
>On earth . . . as it is in heaven.
>Give us this day our daily bread;
>And forgive us . . ."

Hans touches his own heart,

>" . . . our trespasses, as we forgive"

Hans places his hand gently on Todd.

" . . . those who trespass **against us.**"

Todd begins to sob. In the background, Brother Hockstetler, Bishop Anken, and the other Elders enter and come up behind the group at the couch. They, too, kneel silently and listen to Hans.

"And lead us not into **temptation,**
But deliver us from **evil** . . ."

Hans looks upward.

"For **Thine** is the kingdom,
And the power, and the glory,
Forever and **ever** . . .
AMEN."

Todd sobs uncontrollably as he looks at the Amish faces surrounding him. "I'm sorry . . . I'm so sorry I burned your barns."

He gasps for air. "Oh, God, forgive me for everything . . . for lying about . . ."

Just then, in the background through the opening, Royer hurries into the room and pulls up short when he sees the group gathered around Todd, who is still sobbing.

Hurrying across to the couch, Royer bends over next to Todd.

Rebecca is startled at seeing Royer, as are Hans and the children.

Royer, urgent but calmly, speaks to Todd. "You can't keep going on like this, son . . ."

Todd's words now come rushing out. "I did it! It was an *accident!* That Amish kid *didn't kill* my brother."

Rebecca breaks down and tears stream down her cheeks. She silently cries as Todd continues.

"When I fell over the old man, the knife accidentally went into my brother's body, and . . ." Todd's voice chokes and tears stream down his face.

The Elders look at one another, then to Bishop Anken. After a long silence, the Bishop takes a deep breath, then quietly says to the group gathered in the now crowed room, "Brother Matthew has been wrongly judged."

Now frantic, Royer *pleads* to Todd. "Todd, please . . . tell me where you have Alex and Matthew!"

Shocked by his words, Rebecca frantically questions, "Matthew's with you, James Royer!?"

Royer turns to Rebecca and as gently as possible breaks the news to her. "Matthew and Alex were kidnapped, and . . ."

There is a gasp from everyone. Rebecca can only repeat, panicked, "*KIDNAPPED!?*"

Just then, from overhead, they hear a tremendous roar from a helicopter as it descends, shaking the house. A bullhorn calls out with Darren's voice, "Chief! Chief Royer! We need to see you . . ."

Royer starts to get up when Todd reaches out and touches his arm. "They were at the bridge . . . I tried to help them."

As the impact of Todd's words sink in, Royer, heartsick, gets up and heads for the door. He turns to the Elders. "See if you can find something to carry him. He needs a hospital."

Royer hurries out of the Ammann house to the front yard, quickly followed by Rebecca, Hans, and the children, just as the helicopter lands in front of the pond.

The motor shuts off and as the blades slow down, Darren looks across to Royer and speaks through the bullhorn. "We found them trapped under a piece of wreckage."

Alex, in her torn and muddy nightshirt, gets out of the helicopter followed by Matthew. He is still barefoot and in his longjohns, and ripped, baggy black pants. They present quite a picture as they look across at the relieved faces of Rebecca, Royer, Hans, and the children.

Alex rushes into Royer's outstretched arms, crying, "I thought you were dead, *Big Guy* . . . I thought you were dead!"

Matthew runs to Rebecca, who practically lifts her son off the ground with her hug as Elizabeth, Mary, and Jacob cling to both of them.

Weary but relieved, Matthew happily responds, "Oh, Mother . . ."

Rebecca rocks him in her arms reassuringly. "It's over, Matthew. You're safe now."

Just then, Hockstetler, Bishop Anken, and the two Elders carry Todd out of the house on a makeshift litter of blankets. Darren approaches from the helicopter.

Royer takes a step toward Todd as the Elders stop. He turns to Darren and says wearily, "Take him to the Naval Hospital at Bethesda, and call the Admiral."

Darren responds obediently, "Yes, sir!"

Looking down at Todd, Royer gently speaks to him. "The last thing your father said to me was, 'Royer . . . try to bring him in alive. He's all I have left.' . . . and I'm keeping my promise."

Looking up and with a tear in his voice Todd asks, "Did he really say that?"

Royer, reaching out and touching his arm, responds, "He sure as hell did."

As the Elders start to take Todd to the helicopter, they pass between Matthew and Alex. Todd apologetically looks up at their faces and they look down at him with compassion.

Matthew reaches down and gently presses the pocketknife into Todd's hand. "Thanks."

Royer turns back to Alex. "Let's go home. Your mother is waiting for us." He slips his arm behind her and they begin walking toward the helicopter.

Matthew takes a step forward and starts to speak. "I . . ." He's too choked up to continue.

With a longing, Royer puts his arm around him. "Me, too, son."

Royer then takes a quick glance at Rebecca and their eyes meet in the oneness of their thoughts.

Finally, Rebecca speaks. "God bless you, James Royer."

"You, too, Rebecca. Have a good life."

He turns and takes Alex's arm and leads her to the helicopter.

Hans moves up next to Rebecca as she gathers her children to her.

In the background, Alex looks back and sees one of the arriving neighbors, a beautiful young Amish girl, running toward them.

It is Sarah. She rushes up to Matthew, breathless but relieved. "Matthew! Matthew! I'm so glad you're home again."

Matthew acknowledges her with a concerned nod but continues to look at Alex and Royer approaching the helicopter. Alex, about to get in, pauses and looks back once again at Matthew.

Matthew, anxious and frustrated, breaks away from Sarah and his family and runs over to Alex.

They look at each other. Alex, with sadness in her eyes, but trying to be light, speaks first. "Next time, I'll bring the bundling board (her eyes start to tear), and *YOU* bring the flashlight!"

Turning, she quickly gets in. With a deep sigh, Matthew, *knowing it can never be,* silently walks back to his family and Sarah.

Royer, before climbing in, looks at Hans and his family.

Hans gently speaks. "Thank you, James Royer."

After a long moment, Royer gives Hans a nod and gets in. The door closes and the helicopter takes off.

Rebecca, Hans, Matthew, and the children watch as the craft ascends.

The helicopter disappears into the breaking dawn and over the rise of the hill, silhouetting the departing Amish buggies in the morning sun.

Letter to the Reader

Dear Reader:

Upon finishing a book one can't help but have a mental picture of who would be ideal to play the various actors if it was made into a *motion picture.*

Here's your chance to possibly influence the casting of the different roles as they fit into *your* imagination.

Why not take a stab at playing "CASTING DIRECTOR" and send back your choices on the self-addressed card attached on the following page.

We welcome your suggestions and hope you enjoyed reading *Dichotomy ♦ Amish Justice!*

Sincerely,

Beverley and Stan Jolley

CASTING SUGGESTIONS

Royer   _____

Rebecca   _____

Matthew   _____

Katherine   _____

Alex   _____

Hans   _____

Todd   _____

Dino   _____

Ezra   _____

Amos   _____

Sarah   _____

BUSINESS REPLY MAIL

FIRST-CLASS MAIL PERMIT NO. 323 WOODLAND HILLS, CA

POSTAGE WILL BE PAID BY ADDRESSEE

PENN PRESS
PMB 291
22106 CLARENDON ST
WOODLAND HILLS, CA 91367-9780

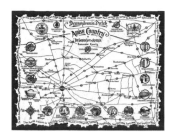 

P.S. DEAR READER:

After working weeks with sepia pen and ink while creating the AMISH "MAP" and "MURAL," I thought some of you might like to have a LITHOGRAPH of the *original artwork*, which is 18 ³/4" high x 23 ³/4" wide on parchment-like cover paper and ready for framing.

If interested, please indicate your choice, or choices, and return the order form shown below with your check payable to:

PENN PRESS
PMB 291   Sincerely,
22106 Clarendon St.   Stan Jolley
Woodland Hills, CA 91367-9780

Amish "MAP"   _____$15.00
Amish "MURAL"   _____$15.00
Both "MAP" & "MURAL"   _____$25.00

Name: _____

Address: _____

_____

_____

Zip Code _____

Please allow $3.50 for postage and handling charges.

Order Information

Obtain "DICHOTOMY ♦ *AMISH JUSTICE!" from your favorite bookstore.*

If your bookstore does not have it in stock, you can order it directly for $21.95 plus $3.00 for shipping and handling per book. If five or more copies are ordered, send only $2.00 for shipping and handling per book.

Mail order blank with check or money order payable to:
PENN PRESS
PMB 291
22106 Clarendon St.
Woodland Hills, CA 91367-9780

"DICHOTOMY ♦ AMISH JUSTICE!"

Number of books requested: _____

Total Enclosed: _____

Mailing Address:

Name: _____

Address & Zip Code: _____

_____

Autograph requests: TO... _____

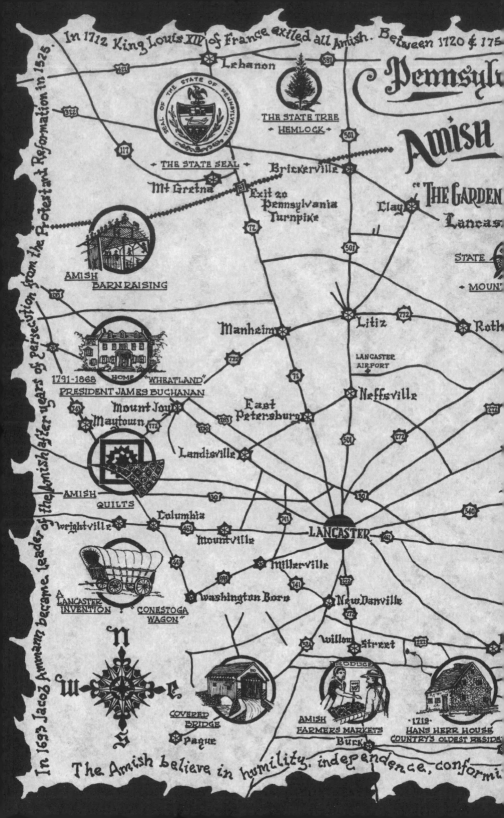

In 1712 King Louis XIV of France exiled all Amish. Between 1720 & 175_

In 1693 Jacob Ammann became leader of the Amish after years of persecution from the Protestant Reformation in 1525.

Pennsylv_

AMISH

"THE GARDEN

Lancas_

STATE _

MOUN'

THE STATE TREE
HEMLOCK

THE STATE OF PENNSYLVANIA

THE STATE SEAL

Lebanon

Brickerville

Clay

Mt Gretna

Exit 20
Pennsylvania
Turnpike

AMISH
BARN RAISING

Manheim

Litiz

Roth_

LANCASTER
AIRPORT

Neffsville

1791-1868
HOME "WHEATLAND"
PRESIDENT JAMES BUCHANAN

Mount Joy

East
Petersburg

Maytown

Landisville

AMISH
QUILTS

Columbia

Wrightville

Mountville

LANCASTER

Millerville

A
LANCASTER
INVENTION
"CONESTOGA
WAGON"

Washington Born

New Danville

Willow Street

N

W   E

S

COVERED
BRIDGE

Paque

AMISH
FARMERS MARKETS

Burk_

1719
HANS HERR HOUSE
COUNTRY'S OLDEST RESIDE_

The Amish believe in humility, independence, conformi_